RETHINKING LEADERSHIP AND "WHOLE OF GOVERNMENT" NATIONAL SECURITY REFORM: PROBLEMS, PROGRESS, AND PROSPECTS

Joseph R. Cerami
Jeffrey A. Engel
Editors

May 2010

*****

Published by Books Express Publishing
Books Express, 2011
ISBN 978-1-780395-21-0

Books Express publications are available from all good retail and online booksellers. For
publishing proposals and direct ordering please contact us at: info@books-express.com

CONTENTS

FOREWORD

On June 24, 2009, The Bush School of Government and Public Service and The Scowcroft Institute of International Affairs at Texas A&M University, and the U. S. Army War College, Strategic Studies Institute (SSI), conducted a conference on "Leadership and Government Reform" in Washington, DC. Two panels discussed Leader Development in Schools of Public Affairs and Leadership, National Security, and "Whole of Government" Reforms.

This conference marked the fourth in a series that the Bush School has conducted with the SSI. The first, "The Future of Transatlantic Security Relations," was held in 2006; the second, "The Interagency and Counterinsurgency Warfare," in 2007. In March 2008, the Bush School conducted a colloquium in College Station, Texas, focused on "Reform and the Next President's Agenda," which looked forward to the November 2008 election. That conference was also sponsored by the nonpartisan Project on National Security Reform, which includes retired Lieutenant General Brent Scowcroft as a member of its Guiding Coalition that originally included several key members of the Obama administration.

The June 24 conference theme continued the discussion about the need for changes in leader development and whole of government reform—even more reform than the post-World War II changes accomplished by the 1947 National Security Act and the 1986 Goldwater-Nichols legislation. The chapters here examine whether and to what extent it is possible to boldly and fundamentally improve the alignment, coordination, integration, and interoperability among the government's national security agencies.

The panelists and authors have reflected on the nature of external, internal, and transnational threats to U.S. security, and the needs for changes in developing people, organizations, and institutions to more effectively, efficiently, and ethically improve the U.S. Government's capacity to address the need for change. In essence, the authors in this book share the belief of many in the international and public affairs community, such as Brent Scowcroft and Zbigniew Brzezinski, that the world is changing in fundamental ways, and our traditional models for understanding America's role do not appear to be working very well.[1] A new era of reform is needed for this new age, in response to which the panelists, in their detailed remarks[2] and subsequent papers, offer suggestions to reform the United States' national security system to meet 21st century threats, while simultaneously developing the leaders who can implement a serious and broad-scale reform agenda.

The SSI joins the coeditors of this volume in thanking the Bush School staff members for their superb efforts in planning and executing the conference, and in preparing this volume. Beth Roberts, Mary Hein, Matthew Upton, Joe Dillard, and Laura Templeton provided the excellent support needed for the conference planning and execution. They were joined by Lindsey Pavelka, who also contributed to the initial SSI conference Colloquium Brief. Matt Henderson video-taped the DC conference and edited the videos which have been posted on the Bush School and the SSI website. Ethan Bennett provided research assistance and his considerable writing skills in preparing the chapters presented in this volume. We thank them and the Bush School's former Dean, Lieutenant General Richard A. Chilcoat (USA, Ret.), Interim Dean, Dr. A. Benton Cocanaugher, Executive Associate Dean, Dr. Sam Kirkpatrick, and Master's Degree Program Directors, Dr. Charles Hermann and Dr. Jeryl L. Mumpower, for their leadership in promoting a significant and continuing partnership with the SSI.

DOUGLAS C. LOVELACE, JR.
Director
Strategic Studies Institute

ENDNOTES - FOREWORD

1. Zbigniew Brzezinski and Brent Scowcroft, *America and the World: Conversations on the Future of American Foreign Policy,* New York: Basic Books, 2008, p. viii.

2. For Leadership and Government Reform conference panelists' videos on June 24, 2009, see *bush.tamu.edu/DC2009/.*

CHAPTER 1

WILL WHAT WE THINK WE KNOW ABOUT LEADERSHIP AND "WHOLE OF GOVERNMENT" REFORM KILL THE PROSPECTS FOR EFFECTIVE AND ETHICAL CHANGE?[1]

Joseph R. Cerami[2]

> The end of man is knowledge, but there is one thing he can't know. He can't know whether knowledge will save him or kill him. He will be killed, all right, but he can't know whether he is killed because of the knowledge which he has got or because of the knowledge which he hasn't got and which if he had it, would save him. . . . for the end of man is to know.
>
> Robert Penn Warren
> *All the King's Men*[3]

On June 24, 2009, the Bush School of Government and Public Service and Scowcroft Institute of International Affairs at Texas A&M University, and the Strategic Studies Institute at the U. S. Army War College, conducted a conference on "Leadership and Government Reform" in Washington, DC. One of two panels discussed "Leader Development in Schools of Public Affairs," the second discussed "Leadership, National Security, and 'Whole of Government' Reforms."

The Bush School's mission statement emphasizes preparing principled leaders for public service, leadership for people, organizations, and institutions that serve the public interest. To think more broadly about leadership and government reform, the panels were challenged to think about the whole of government rather than leadership at the top, or solely on the role of presidential leadership. The aim was to think more about government reform and leadership from the top, middle and entry levels.

The authors of this book share the viewpoint of many in the international and public affairs community that the world is changing, and our theories, concepts, and practices for understanding America's role and implementing effective and ethical policies do not seem to be working very well.[4] Is a new era of reform needed for this new age? Can we offer concrete as well as theoretical suggestions to reform the U.S. national security system to meet 21st century threats? Do we also know how to develop the kind of effective and ethical leaders who can make such reforms work? The chapters in this volume address these pressing and timely issues.

PANEL 1: INTRODUCTION—LEADER DEVELOPMENT IN SCHOOLS OF PUBLIC AND INTERNATIONAL AFFAIRS

In introducing the first panel, Dr. Joseph Cerami commented on the Bush School graduate program's approach to leader development, an approach tailored for a school of public and international affairs. One guiding idea is that leadership education is integrated into the 2-year program and not viewed as a stand-alone activity. The Bush School emphasizes leadership and teamwork starting with its admissions process and candidate interview weekend and during new student orientation week. Every master's candidate takes a core graduate-level leadership course. These activities early in the Bush School experience contribute to establishing class identities and reinforce a commitment to personal and professional leader development.

From there, the School supports student efforts through individual learning and leader development, and recommends that students design their course work to provide a base of knowledge and skills as a foundation for their desired career paths. These efforts are guided by coaching from faculty advisers, and supplemented with the opportunities to interact frequently with a diverse group of experienced practitioners, faculty experts, and visiting speakers. The students' final core course is a team-based Capstone research project under faculty direction for a real-world client.

In addition to course work, the Bush School also emphasizes two additional layers, including experiential learning through leadership positions in the student government association, public service organization, intramurals, internships, and community service. The third layer includes personal development or self-study. Ms. Lindsey Pavelka, the Assistant Leadership Director, directs an assessment center whose menu of tools for improving self-awareness includes online assessments of personality profiles (Myers-Briggs Type Indicator), individual learning styles, a personal assessment of management skills, personal values assessments, and emotion intelligence.

The Panelists: Erik Patashnik, Joel Rosenthal, and Todd Pittinsky.

Panel 1 included three individuals who are deeply concerned with education, leader development, public policy, international affairs, and ethics. Their publications, teaching, and—very importantly—their institutions, are all committed to promoting the cause of student development and public service.

Dr. Eric Patashnik has written extensively on government reform, performance, and public administration and management. Dr. Patashnik discussed his work as Associate Director in establishing the Batten School of Leadership and Public Policy at the University of Virginia, where they believe there is an academic component for integrating leadership and public policy. In the course of the Batten School's dean search, he compiled a list of ideas their finalists shared about the need for integrating leadership and public policy. Those ideas emphasized efforts to:

1. Feature courses that bring together leadership and public policy through successful and failed cases of change management and innovation,
2. Emphasize leadership across policy networks,
3. Understand a variety of leadership roles along with the significance of context and leading at different organizational levels,
4. Focus on leadership successes rather than just distilling lessons from failures,
5. Teach followership skills, emphasizing listening, feedback, and challenging behaviors,
6. Think about leadership in a number of courses, not just one course, and weave leadership studies throughout the curriculum,
7. Break down the concept of leadership into discrete, teachable skills (speaking, writing, missions, crisis, negotiations, etc.),
8. Recognize differences in backgrounds of students by differentiating the curriculum,
9. Reimagine the field of leadership by engaging with other social science disciplines,
10. Consider leadership in student admissions selection criteria, and

11. Define leadership broadly so all faculty and students can see their connections to the field.

Dr. Todd Pittinsky is the Research Director for Harvard Kennedy School's Center for Public Leadership. The Center for Public Leadership (CPL) webpage notes that the Center is:

> Dedicated to excellence in leadership education and research. . .by creating opportunities for reflection and discovery for students, scholars, and practitioners from different disciplines, sectors, cultures, and nations [thus promoting] a dynamic exchange of ideas.

Pittinsky introduced his research on leading across boundaries and intergroup leadership. He suggested that by focusing on collective identity, i.e., taking a group of different individuals and finding commonalities between them, groups will discover ways to integrate their strengths rather than focusing solely on who they are as individuals. He elaborated on collective identity, emphasizing the abundance of knowledge about the repulsion of different groups, but the lack of knowledge about the groups' attraction. Todd suggested that society has a natural tendency to think in terms of categories, looking at differences as "us and them." He encouraged the idea of leading-by-uniting, and the advantages of looking at shared identities or commonalities between seemingly very different groups.

The third panelist was Dr. Joel Rosenthal of the Carnegie Council for Ethics in International Affairs. The Carnegie Council has been hosting U.S. Army War College small group visits to Carnegie, New York, and conducts faculty workshops there on Humanitarian Interventions and other topics regarding the military, international affairs, and ethical leadership. As its webpage says, "The Carnegie Council is the world's leading voice promoting ethical leadership on issues of war, peace, and global social justice." Rosenthal explored the connection between ethics and leadership, suggesting that there is a need for schools of public affairs to follow the suit of other professional schools, like business, medicine, etc., which offer separate courses on ethics. Rosenthal set the stage for ethics as a process of reflection about how we should live — our values, standards, and principles — then shared what he referred to as three-dimensional ethics. The first dimension, ethics as choice, emphasized the role individuals who have autonomy in an organization play in setting ethical standards. The second dimension, systems and social arrangements, determines the kinds of choices individuals make. The third dimension, the opportunity to imagine and implement new social arrangements, provides an unconventional way of thinking about ethics. Referring to a previous panelist's comments and the Bush School's mission of preparing principled leaders, Rosenthal prompted the question: "What is principled leadership?" He suggested three ideas at its core: (1) pluralism, an appreciation for diversity while exercising what is common in the human condition, (2) principles of rights, what he referred to as the "rock bottom moral argument," and (3) fairness. In summary, Rosenthal emphasized the importance and moral obligation we have to continuously discuss and study ethics, which he suggests should be seen as "the rudder and keel — the things that keep one moving forward and in the right direction."

PANEL 2: INTRODUCTION — LEADERSHIP, NATIONAL SECURITY, AND WHOLE OF GOVERNMENT REFORM

The second panel, led by Dr. Jeffrey Engel, the Interim Director of the Scowcroft Institute of International Affairs, explored the role of leadership and whole of government reform in the areas of national security, homeland security, foreign policy, and intelligence. Surely there has been no lack of attention to these areas of government since September 11, 2001 (9/11), and indeed since the end of the Cold War that preceded it. The current Obama administration made national security reform, both in tone and in practice, one of the signatures of its electoral campaign. As several speakers noted, however, such emphasis on reform was meant more for public consumption than for actual bureaucratic reorganization, which is hardly a new phenomenon in American electoral politics. The panelists charged with addressing this vital topic of national security reform included academics, practitioners, historians, and contemporary policy analysts.

The Panelists: Geoffrey French, James Goldgeier, Richard Immerman, and Andrew Preston.

The panel began with Mr. Geoffrey French, Analytic Director of Security Risk for CENTRA Technology, Inc., a leading contractor in the area of homeland security and risk analysis for the U.S. Government, particularly for the Departments of Homeland Security, Defense, and the Federal Bureau of Investigation. French opened the discussion of leadership, national security, and government reform by focusing on homeland security and intelligence. He emphasized the need to consolidate current forums and functions and avoid duplicating mechanisms for information sharing. He suggested focusing on fusion centers as the forum for information exchange and the need for common terminology to connect homeland security and intelligence agencies. In concluding his arguments, French emphasized the notion that if homeland security intelligence exists, then so too should the nation improve its homeland security counterintelligence.

Next to speak was Dr. James Goldgeier of the George Washington University's Elliot School of International Affairs and the Council on Foreign Relations, who addressed the role of ideology and worldview in shaping American foreign policy since the end of the Cold War. He also discussed the way that worldview in turn framed the range of possible avenues of reform for the Clinton, George W. Bush, and now Obama administrations. Goldgeier's comments on international security were supported by his recent research focus on the transition from the end of the Cold War to the post-Cold War periods. In particular, he mentioned contending ideas on America's post-Cold War role. Examples included the debate between the 1992 draft Defense Planning guidance of Richard Cheney and Paul Wolfowitz, and the January 1993 State Department document by Secretary Lawrence Eagleburger about the significance of the global economy and the need to develop a National Economic Council to complement the work of the National Security Council (NSC). Goldgeier also addressed the need for training public and international affairs professionals in the new forces at work in economics, energy, and cyber policy areas.

Dr. Richard Immerman of Temple University, and more recently of the Directorate of National Intelligence, then spoke on the myriad ways academic and intellectually-informed ideas about how reform within the intelligence community (in particular following 9/11 and the Iraq War) did or did not succeed in practice. His lesson: given that reform is hard, even for the most well-intentioned, we should be giving more attention to current history to critically examine the details of intelligence reform. He provided a narrative on what he evaluates as an important reform effort undertaken by the Director of National Intelligence, focussing on institutional initiatives. In particular, he reinforced the significance of the initiatives by Tom Fingar of the Directorate of National Intelligence, who challenged the intelligence analytical community to reform, embrace change, and lead the development of a community of intelligence analysts. Fingar's guiding assumption was that there would always be gaps in analysis; therefore, the intelligence community needed analysts with the judgment to help bridge those gaps. In addition, he suggested that the intelligence community needed educational reforms to address critical thinking skills and standards. Also needed was a library of national intelligence to provide a knowledge base of all reports. Other initiatives included designing an A-Space, classified, social network to join all officials in the analysis and collection agencies for collaboration. Immerman concluded with the optimistic assessment that, through diligent effort and despite long-standing bureaucratic inertia and opposition to collaboration and change, reform is indeed possible if leaders desire it and persist in pressing the issue.

Dr. Andrew Preston of Cambridge University concluded the panel. As a leading historian of the McGeorge Bundy era at the NSC and thus of reforms in the transition between the Eisenhower and Kennedy administrations, Preston is uniquely positioned to comment on the similarity of reformist impulses now and in the past. His conclusion: a more recent perspective on reform, specifically that orchestrated by Brent Scowcroft during his second term as National Security Adviser (under George H.W. Bush) provides the preferable model by which other reformers might learn. Preston addressed concerns about the NSC, in particular the National Security Adviser, who is often cited as needing reform. The speaker pointed out that every president tries to reform the system, but stressed that he does not see a need for reform now. In fact, he emphasized how current administrations are strikingly similar to that of Bundy's NSC during the Kennedy administration, which he believes "got it right." He mentioned the key Bundy innovation as being the heightened significance of the presidential advisory role (in addition to managing the national security policy process). The speaker also recognized the Bundy concept of the NSC operating like a small State Department, a practice perfected by Scowcroft, whom Preston assesses as unquestionably the most effective national security adviser in U.S. history.

THE CHAPTERS

This anthology continues the conference discussions on the topic of whole of government reform and the role graduate policy programs in public and international affairs play in preparing emerging leaders to participate in ongoing reform processes. There is a large amount of literature on reform and innovation efforts. Much of the research describes the obstacles to whole system reforms in the public and private sectors. In the private sector, John Kotter of Harvard

Business School informs us that most large-scale transformations fail.[5] Kotter points out that "powerful macroeconomic forces are at work" and will continue to push organizational change. Overall, his assessment of change management efforts is not encouraging:

> To date, major change efforts have helped some organizations adapt significantly to shifting conditions, have improved the competitive standing of others, and have positioned a few for a far better future. But in too many situations the improvements have been disappointing and the carnage has been appalling, with wasted resources and burn-out, scared or frustrated employees.[6]

In the government sector, public management scholars continue to assign Charles Lindblom's classic article, "The Science of 'Muddling Through" (1959). Lindblom compares what he calls root (rational-comprehensive) and branch (successive limited comparisons) to "describe policy formulation . . . for complex problems."[7] Lindblom concludes that in the "rough" policymaking process, the branch approach is the way to go: "Policy-making is a process of successive approximation to some desired objectives in which what is desired itself continues to change under reconsideration."[8] To a seasoned practitioner, does change through successive approximation sound like more practical advice than going for reforming the whole of government? Has the base of our knowledge been expanded to the point that we know more about leading and change than the past research of Lindblom and Kotter suggest? In sum, what do we know now that gives us greater confidence in our ability to change or even transform national security organizations and policymaking processes in a single decisive stroke as opposed to an open-ended process of continuous incremental adjustments? While acknowledging the inherent complexities in light of the turbulence in international, domestic, and transnational issues facing the U.S. Government in the coming decades, the following chapters are more positive about recent, ongoing, and future reform efforts than is suggested by the classic research of Kotter, Lindblom, and others.

James Locher's chapter provides a perspective on national security reform (PNSR) that has, in large part, sparked the whole of government initiative.[9] Locher pulls no punches in criticizing an outdated national security system that is ineffective in responding to current threats. Drawing on research from more than 300 experts, PNSR's December 2008 report, "Forging a New Shield," emphasizes the lack of a systems approach for developing strategies; a limited capability for effective complex contingency operations; limited flexibility and untimely decisionmaking and analysis; and lack of overall unity of effort among policymakers and agencies.

Locher identifies five persistent government problems in the current national security system:

1. Autonomous agencies (the Stovepipe Syndrome) defy a unity of effort approach.
2. Major areas of NSC responsibilities are not under the NSC adviser's authority.
3. The White House is overburdened by centralized issue management that is made necessary by a lack of interagency coordination and integration.
4. Resources are not aligned with strategic objectives due to the agency focus on human capital and budget resources.
5. The structure of congressional committees causes a focus on parts of the process, thus

failing to provide legislative initiatives for a whole of government approach.

This list of deficiencies, as well as ideas for addressing them, is presented in more detail in the *Forging a New Shield* report that includes historical case studies adding depth to our understanding of the long-term and persistent nature of these problems in U.S. history.[10] In sum, PNSR's way ahead includes efforts to better integrate the U.S. instruments of national power as well as to create and empower leaders throughout the national security system.

In assessing the early Obama administration, Locher sees forward movement in pursuing the reform agenda. He notes that the national and homeland security functions have been integrated in the NSC.[11] Locher advises that the President create flexible, collaborative teams for decentralized management through interagency panels. In addition, PNSR recommends empowering leaders through human capital incentives for interagency service. To lead the necessary reforms, Locher calls for creating an executive secretary on the NSC staff to form a human capital advisory board; assist the president in creating interagency teams; establish a national security professional corps that provides incentives for interagency rotation; and create a central staff for developing and coordinating interagency professional education, training, and certification programs. In contrast to Lindblom, Locher cites the 9/11 Commission Report stressing that Americans should not settle for ad hoc, incremental change.

Joel Rosenthal's chapter focuses on leadership as practical ethics. He emphasizes the central role of ethics in leadership education and training for anyone with careers in public and international affairs. He also urges fighting the minimalist approach of equating ethics with mere legal compliance, making the case for developing a deep understanding of values, standards of ethical behavior, principles that guide choice, and norms, expectations, ethical claims, and contexts. While noting Isaiah Berlin's warning that normative inquiry is a nonperfectionist's art, he offers a practical, three-dimensional approach to ethical reasoning, including (1) understanding decisonmakers as ethical actors; (2) systems that define the range of choices that address an ethical analysis of the existing rules of the game, as well as practicable norms and expectations; and (3) a conviction that ethical reasoning can improve the situation, and that analysts and decisonmakers can do better in addressing the inevitable dilemma of all real world situations where values come into conflict.

Rosenthal claims a realist international relations worldview in terms of ethics that are grounded in a sense of how things really work, or practical ideas and actions that are built on a foundation of supporting values. In short, ethical leadership includes a perspective of enlightened self-interest. To assist in ethical thinking, Rosenthal constructs an ethical framework that includes three overarching principles: pluralism, rights, and fairness. Building on the legacy of moral realist Reinhold Niebuhr, Rosenthal points out that his approach is not utopian, but rather views individual interests in "terms of complex, interdependence, international norms and global responsibilities."[12] Creating an ethics factor for inclusion in the wide variety of decision matrices and other analytical tools remains wise, if time-consuming, projects for analysts, planners, and decisonmakers. When was the last a time an options paper, think piece, or course-of-action analysis included a discussion of the pros and cons of various options in terms of whether one option is more ethical than another as a selection criterion? Rosenthal's ethical realism provides an important approach to consider both for educating emerging leaders in ethical thinking, and for using ethics to raise important questions about the selection criteria in policy and decisionmaking.

Todd Pittinsky's chapter addresses what we know, or do not really know, about what it means to "win hearts and minds." Pittinsky asks fundamental questions about the nature of what is commonly termed a "soft power" approach to addressing current and diverse issues such counterterrorism, counterinsurgency, democratization, and global warming. In brief, he asks whether we know what an approach for winning hearts and minds can do, who can do it, and what can be done? He also portrays understanding hearts and minds as a fundamental leadership task. The essence of leadership in winning hearts and minds, in this view, is to guide people who may not normally or necessarily want to follow. This would include, for example, leading defeated opponents such as Germany and Japan after World War II.

Reflecting generally on the past 50 years of social science research on group behavior, Pittinsky points out that related studies have focused on overcoming biases and discriminatory practices, especially in the U.S. social context. In other words, research has focused on getting groups to hate each other less but not on suggesting ways to persuade them to like each other more. He introduces the term "allophilia," or the study of how to generate positive feelings about groups that are different from one's own. Pittinsky points out the need for many more cross-national studies to examine the potential for building effective practices for winning hearts and minds across cultures and in a variety of contexts, including conflict and post-conflict environments.

In examining the next phase of homeland security intelligence, Geoffrey French commends the importance of better definitions, roles, and protections, especially in overcoming the pre-9/11 breakdowns between foreign and domestic intelligence. In the case of homeland security legislation, Congress has been very active in initiating legislation that the homeland security and intelligence communities are still interpreting and implementing. The legislative package that French cites includes the USA Patriot Act of 2001, the Homeland Security Act of 2002, the Intelligence Reform and Terrorist Prevention Act of 2004, and the Implementation Recommendations of the 9/11 Commission Act (the 9/11 Act) of 2007. In addition, Congress has mandated new agencies such as the Department of Homeland Security and the National Counterterrorism Center. Perceiving even more complexity, French notes the difficulties involved in applying homeland security reforms in light of the wide array of stakeholders involved, including foreign, military, and homeland intelligence agencies; the federal-state-local government agencies; tribal governments; the owners and operators of the nation's mostly privately-held critical infrastructure; and the public.

French offers several suggestions to address homeland security reform, including the need for a framework for information sharing that includes strategic, risk-based decisionmaking analytical tools and a homeland security-based research and reporting structure similar to the military's intelligence preparation of the battlefield in order to analyze a wide variety of threats to the U.S. homeland. These threats include cases of terrorist and criminal intelligence networks that seek to infiltrate U.S. agencies operating overseas, as well as within the United States. Therefore, he urges the development of the field of U.S. homeland security counterintelligence to thwart the efforts of foreign intelligence agents, terrorists, and criminal gangs.

In French's assessment of ongoing homeland security initiatives, he notes two reform phases in the post-9/11 period. Phase I included the immediate legislative and organizational reforms that filled the gap between domestic and foreign intelligence. He grades Phase I as being largely completed, while allowing that a degree of organizational overlap remains in clarifying the roles and responsibilities of the Department of Homeland Security, the Federal Bureau of Investigation, and the National Counterterrorism Threat Center. No doubt those relations will continue to evolve over time. French believes that we are now in Phase II with the need to clarify the mechanisms for collective processing and sharing of intelligence; to improve communications for risk-based decisionmaking across government agencies at all levels; and to generate new organizations and programs for counterintelligence support and protection. The immediate leadership challenge is to complete timely changes for reforms without the heedless urgency and sometimes erratic approaches caused by the panicky fear of a future homeland security disaster. Reform without the sky-falling platform of another 9/11 requires leadership that embraces homeland security professionals, Congress, and government agencies, as well as public organizations and citizens. Effective homeland security reform that is not driven for its own sake and not by the specter of a second 9/11 "failure" remains a challenge, especially as memories of 9/11 fade after what will soon be 10 years without an attack on U.S. territory.

Turning to American foreign policy, James Goldgeier addresses the need for reform in a globalizing war. Building on his previous research on the transition between the Cold War and the early post-Cold War decade of the 1990s, he points out the end of the distinctions between the high politics issues of superpower relations, nuclear deterrence, containment, and crisis management on one hand, and the low politics of third world development, international economics, and environmental issues on the other.

Goldgeier highlights the struggle to define the direction for the post-Cold War guiding strategy by contrasting two competing visions at the end of the George H. W. Bush administration. He compares divergent worldviews in the January 1993 draft Defense Planning Guidance document that outlined the need for U.S. primacy in Europe and Asia, with a State Department transition memorandum that highlighted the new security challenges of transnational threats. So the stark choice between a traditional great power approach to international politics and that of a fresh perspective on the nature of globalization, especially in international economics and humanitarian interventions, faced the incoming Clinton administration. The latter approach fit the Clinton worldview, and Goldgeier argues that from that point forward, probably more so than at any time since the post-World War II Marshall Plan, the United States embarked on a foreign policy that was mainly about economic policy. That decision in turn led to the formation of the National Economic Council, with a new more important international role for Treasury Secretaries with Wall Street and economic backgrounds as exemplified by

Robert Rubin and Larry Summers. In the international context, Goldgeier also points to the ascendancy of international economic organizations, such as the International Monetary Fund, over bilateral ties. In sum, during the Clinton era, international economic institutions came to trump national security and foreign policy agencies, while international and domestic economic issues came to trump national security policy.

In the post-9/11 era of the George W. Bush administration, Goldgeier sees a redirection back to the predominance of national security issues and the decline in the status of such Treasury Secretaries as Paul O'Neill and John Snow along with the relative decline in clout and influence of the National Economic Council. This shift in foreign policymaking continued until the financial meltdown of 2008. Goldgeier sees the pendulum for the Obama administration as swinging back towards the Clinton worldview. Evidence of this can be seen in a memorandum by Obama national security adviser, Retired Marine Corps General James Jones, echoing Locher's concerns that the national security organizations' ability to respond to global challenges is "inadequate or deficient." Jones emphasizes the nature of emerging transnational threats, the significance of international economics, as well as the need for expanding the whole of government's policymaking capacity. Goldgeier highlights the current NSC needs for all cabinet and related agencies to have someone in the front office with an NSC portfolio to work more directly at the NSC staff level; a cyber czar; a new China policy that integrates strategic and economic issues; and a deputy national security adviser for international economic affairs.

Goldgeier's early assessment is that the Obama administration has shifted back to the Clintonian approach to international leadership and will reform the NSC by reorienting policy priorities and reconnecting international political and economic affairs. This in turn will require agency chiefs such as Secretaries of State George Schultz and James Baker with economics and business experience. At the same time, for balanced policymaking, Goldgeier sees the need for national security experts to work at Treasury and the National Economic Council and other traditional domestic policy venues.

On a final note, Goldgeier points out a need for students and policymakers grounded in the interdisciplinary knowledge of political science and economics to supply the current and next generation of strategic leaders. He wonders who will write today's equivalent of Bernard Brodie's post-World War II classic, *Strategy in the Missile Age*.[13] Given the rise of Asia, terrorism, weapons of mass destruction (WMD), climate change, and energy as issues of political economy, is educational reform also needed in schools of public and international affairs? Do our policy schools know how to create the interdisciplinary studies, such as international political economy, that are necessary to best prepare emerging leaders to think clearly about strategy in a global age?

Richard Immerman provides the most optimistic narrative of change in his treatment of knowledge management. His case study of the transformation of intelligence analysis provides a first-hand account of his service from 2007 through 2008 as Assistant Deputy Director of National Intelligence for Analytic Integrity and Standards, and as Analytic Ombudsman for the Office of the Director of National Intelligence. As in homeland security reforms post-9/11, Congress initiated reform efforts through the 2004 Intelligence

Reform and Terrorism Prevention Act. The chapter follows Immerman's panel remarks, tracing the efforts at analytic transformation within the intelligence community through education, training, and development of a community of analysts.

Immerman characterizes these reform efforts as "commonsensical," commending the committed leadership and creative approaches. The role of the first Deputy Director for National Intelligence is highlighted, as is the significance of harnessing information technology and social networking to improve the quality of intelligence analysis. Immerman points out that though those initial efforts had to overcome powerful institutional and cultural challenges, the initial results are promising. Adapting similar approaches in other functional areas to bring together communities of experts in real time through education and networking appears to be a commonsensical, but it is an uncommon approach across agencies. Overcoming the obstacles that hinder greater interagency coordination remains a challenge as is pointed out in numerous case studies of national security policymaking throughout U.S. history.

Andrew Preston provides a history of the role of the national security adviser. He agrees with many who point out that the national security adviser serves as the pivot point in all policymaking and in the policy apparatus itself. His main point is that there is an inherent tension between the main roles of the national security adviser, who on one hand should serve as an honest broker in channeling ideas and recommendations to the President and the NSC, while on the other serving at times as a policy advocate.[14] Preston in Chapter 6 of the present anthology characterizes this as a "delicate balancing act."

To provide historical context, Preston highlights the McGeorge Bundy approach under the Kennedy administration as a model, much like that of Brent Scowcroft in the post-Iran Contra era. In sum, the national security adviser must be a thinker and a doer, an intellectual and a bureaucrat. Balancing those roles and assisting the President in fulfilling his national security roles, however, requires more than a wise national security adviser, he must also be an active one.

Preston devotes significant attention to the national security top team, attributing the success of Brent Scowcroft to the efforts of an engaged foreign policy President, George H. W. Bush, as well as an effective deputy, such as Robert Gates.[15] His assessment is that Scowcroft unquestionably ranks as the most effective national security adviser in U.S. history. Preston's early take on the Obama administration is that if current National Security Adviser James Jones ignores the "delicate balance," emphasizing policy management to the exclusion of policy advocacy, he runs the danger of becoming marginalized in national security affairs.

CONCLUDING THOUGHTS

Taken as a whole, the conference panels and the following chapters argue on behalf of the need for government reform. Simultaneously, they argue that collective leadership and individual and group leader development require further emphasis—especially in such areas as political economy, information sharing, and ethics—for any reform to have true meaning. The United States wields the world's largest national security structure. It is spending more on defense than the rest of the world combined in this first decade of the

21st century, plus a prodigious amount (though not wholly publicly divulged) on intelligence and homeland security. While the weight and size of these programs naturally compel critiques, no thoughtful observer disputes the need for a sizable national security apparatus. Yet, by and large, as reformers inside and outside of government point out, America's post 9/11 security agencies and institutions retain their Cold War design. Even with the Cold War having ended more than 20 years ago, the 1947 National Security Act remains the defining charter of the nation's security system.[16]

To address the topic of leadership and government reform, the panelists and the chapters focus on these main research questions:

1. Are graduate programs in schools of public and international affairs paying sufficient attention to the study of leadership and the development of leaders for public service careers? In particular, how are policy schools at the University of Virginia, Harvard University, and Texas A&M University finding new ways to educate future leaders, promote interdisciplinary leadership research, and provide a foundation of knowledge and skills for the next generation of government reformers?
2. Given recent advances in leadership studies, what more remains to be done to improve the ethical education of current and future leaders?
3. To what extent should further attention be paid to the interpersonal and group dynamics of leaders at the nation's highest levels, including the President and his/her upper echelon national security team, whose conscientious

direction remains vital to any meaningful reform and functioning of the nation's security apparatus? How can we draw on history to enlighten such studies of the present and future? While large scale, whole of government reform is regarded as desirable by many scholars and contemporary students of national security policy, is it more reasonable to assume that absent a new confrontation on the order of the Cold War or a crisis rivaling the terrorist attacks of 9/11, incremental change and continuous improvement offer more probable approaches to reform?

4. Have the reforms enacted since the 2001 attacks made significant improvements in transforming the nation's security apparatus from its Cold War framework? While the authors in this anthology and most experts generally agree that more must be done to improve homeland security, intelligence sharing, and counterintelligence coordination, the key concern is if this is possible without simultaneously infringing on civil liberties protections for citizens? Do advances in information technology especially offer opportunities for further integration of the nation's far-flung intelligence community? Should similar effort be made to increase the alignment and coordination among homeland security operatives at the local, state, and federal level, while paying due attention to the increasing role of cyber security; environmental concerns; and economics, trade, and development?

5. Is it possible to approach reform efforts in ways that cannot be politicized? Does past experience

show that true transformation typically occurs not with the aid of foresight, but rather in rash response to a new, unforeseen threat? Do the post-Cold War and post-9/11 periods offer examples of bi-level national security system restructuring processes, with major reform efforts first, and with a second level of improvements then pursued at a slower but more sustainable pace?

6. Is it true that partisanship in this realm can lead only to hasty results of the kind unlikely to prevent future attacks? Is it possible for reformers to operate in a spirit of nonpartisanship in security affairs so that true reform might withstand the knee-jerk desire to enact immediate reform in the aftermath of a future attack?

7. Is real reform best done strategically, progressively, and through leadership that combines expertise and experience with a spirit of change in a manner that is best described as incremental change? Or is whole of government or whole system reform the necessary path to effective change?

The following chapters add to the reform knowledge base by addressing these questions. The panelists and authors have reflected on the nature of external, internal, and transnational threats to U.S. security, and the need for changes in developing people, organizations, and institutions to more effectively, efficiently, and ethically enhance the U.S. Government's capacity to address the need for change. In essence, the authors in this book share the belief of many in the international and public affairs community, such as Brent

Scowcroft and Zbigniew Brzezinski, that "the world is changing in fundamental ways, and . . . our traditional models for understanding America's role don't work very well."[17] A new era of reform is needed for this new age. The panelists, in their detailed remarks[18] and subsequent chapters, offer a host of concrete and theoretical suggestions to reform the U.S. national security system to meet 21st century threats, while simultaneously developing the kind of learned, broadly understanding, and ethical leaders with the knowledge and character necessary to make such reforms work.[19]

ENDNOTES – CHAPTER 1

1. A summary of many of the ideas in this introduction were included in a Strategic Studies Institute (SSI) *Colloquium Brief*, by Joseph R. Cerami, Jeffrey A. Engel, and Lindsey K. Pavelka, available from the SSI website at *www.StrategicStudiesInstitute. army.mil*.

2. The author thanks the SSI for conducting the Leadership and Government Reform conference and for publishing this volume. Professor Douglas Lovelace and Dr. Robin Dorff have provided invaluable advice, support, and friendship for many years. The SSI staff (Ms. Marianne Cowling, Ms. Rita Rummel, Colonel John Dabrowski, and Dr. James Pierce) has always been gracious and patient in providing editorial support in publishing conference reports.

3. Robert Penn Warren, *All The King's Men* (Restored Ed.), New York: Harcourt, Inc., 2001, p. 13.

4. Zbigniew Brzezinski and Brent Scowcroft, *America and the World: Conversations on the Future of American Foreign Policy,* New York: Basic Books, 2008, p. viii.

5. John P. Kotter, *Leading Change,* Boston, MA: Harvard Business School Press, 1996.

6. *Ibid.*, pp. 2-3.

7. Charles E. Lindblom, "The Science of Muddling Through," Jay M. Shafritz and Albert C. Hyde, eds., *Classics of Public Administration*, Third Ed., Belmont, CA: Wadsworth Publishing Company, 1992. Reprinted with permission from *Public Administration Review*.

8. *Ibid.*, p. 232.

9. More information regarding the Project on National Security Reform is available from *www.pnsr.org/index.asp*. In addition, Locher presented a keynote address, "Leadership and the National Security Reform Agenda," at a March 20, 2008, symposium at a SSI-Bush School conference on "Leadership and National Security Reform: The Next President's Agenda." Locher's overview on the PNSR project can be found in the Colloquium Report co-edited by Joseph R. Cerami, Robin Dorff, and Lisa M. Moorman, October 2008, available from *www.StrategicStudiesInstitute.army.mil*.

10. Project on National Security Reform, *Forging a New Shield*, Arlington, VA: November 2008, available from *www.pnsr.org/data/files/pnsr_forging_a_new_shield_report.pdf*.

11. For more details on the NSC structure and functions, see also Presidential Policy Directive-1; "Organization of the National Security Council System," Washington, DC: The White House, February 13, 2009.

12. See Reinhold Niebuhr, *The Irony of American History* (with a new Introduction by Andrew J. Bacevich), Chicago, IL: University of Chicago Press, 2008 (1952). The book jacket blurb by Senator Barack Obama says: "[Niebuhr] is one of my favorite philosophers. I take away [from his works] the compelling idea that there's serious evil in the world, and hardship and pain. And we should be humble and modest in our belief we can eliminate those things. But we shouldn't use that as an excuse for cynicism and inaction."

13. Bernard Brodie, *Strategy in the Missile Age* (The RAND

Corporation), Princeton, NJ: Princeton University Press, 1959.

14. Paul Nitze points to tension as the basis for practical thinking in international politics. He draws his inspiration from the Greek philosopher Heraclitus's assertion that "truth and beauty were to be found in the tension between opposites." Paul H. Nitze, *Tension Between Opposites: Reflections on the Practice and Theory of Politics*, New York: Charles Scribner's Sons, 1993, p. 15.

15. A similar account of the effectiveness of the Bush-Scow-croft-Gates national security team in comparison to other administrations is in David J. Rothkopf, *Running the World: The Inside Story of the National Security Council and The Architects of American Power*, New York: Public Affairs, 2005.

16. Douglas T. Stuart. *Creating the National Security State: A History of the Law That Transformed America*, Princeton, NJ: Princeton University Press, 2008.

17. Brzezinski and Scowcroft, p. viii.

18. For Leadership and Government Reform conference panelists' videos on June 24, 2009, see *bush.tamu.edu/DC2009/*.

19. For an interesting comparison of the ways that people and ideas matter in national security policy and decisionmaking, see the contrasting accounts of the war in Iraq provided by Richard N. Haass, *War of Necessity, War of Choice: A Memoir of Two Iraq Wars*, New York: Simon & Shuster, 2009; and Douglas J. Feith, *War and Decision: Inside the Pentagon at the Dawn of the War on Terrorism*, New York: HarperCollins Publishers, 2008.

CHAPTER 2

LEADERSHIP, NATIONAL SECURITY, AND WHOLE OF GOVERNMENT REFORMS: THE PROJECT ON NATIONAL SECURITY REFORM (PNSR) PERSPECTIVE

James R. Locher III

> Reformers have the idea that change can be achieved by brute sanity.
>
> —George Bernard Shaw[1]

The national security system of the United States is outdated and ineffective in responding to the threats that our country faces today. Terrorism, nuclear proliferation, natural disasters, failed states, piracy, pandemics, and cyber security attacks present a hydra of unpredictable and disparate threats. The 21st century security environment differs significantly from that of the Cold War era which molded and refined current U.S. capabilities. This complex system needs urgent repair, restructuring, and modernization.

The Project on National Security Reform (PNSR) arose to meet this challenge. It has carried out the most comprehensive study of the national security system in American history. This endeavor involved more than 300 experts from think tanks, universities, federal agencies, law firms, and the business community. In December 2008, PNSR published *Forging a New Shield*, which details the deficiencies of the current system and provides ambitious but necessary and viable recommendations for rescuing it.

FLAWS OF THE CURRENT SYSTEM

The current national security system was created in the aftermath of World War II, when President Harry Truman signed the National Security Act of 1947. This structure, though never optimal, worked tolerably well in meeting the core challenges of the Cold War. Nonetheless, the current national security system was optimized to overcome post-World War II threats. In the 21st century, it has shown its age. The United States has repeatedly failed to integrate diplomatic, military, economic, and other elements of national power adequately, primarily because various national security organizations are poorly structured to collaborate. We need a new system that is guided by a unified set of goals, integrated in the effective pursuit of these goals, and led by leaders unhindered by wasteful interagency competition or bureaucracy.

Bradley Patterson, a long-time participant in White House operations, describes the importance of interagency cooperation in national security policymaking and execution: for example, assume that the President is going to travel to Moscow to try to persuade the Russian President to collaborate on a missile defense arrangement. Military options and background must be elicited from Defense; diplomatic repercussions evaluated by State; assessments on Russian capabilities will come from the intelligence community; while the White House National Security Council (NSC) staff will assemble the material.[2] As this example illustrates, some national-level organizations have their own domains of expertise; others, like the NSC, integrate their efforts — or are supposed to.

Unfortunately, the current system offers insufficient incentives for such interagency cooperation. Each agency typically uses its capabilities and resources to pursue its own goals and projects. The resultant systemic inability to create and support centrally established missions forces an overburdened President to oversee tasks which could be more efficiently managed elsewhere.

PNSR's comprehensive analysis of past case studies of national security decisions and policies indicates that:

- The U.S. national security apparatus lacks an effective system for developing strategies that connect available resources, desired end states, and implementation procedures.
- Complex contingencies are undertaken without requisite capabilities.
- Rigid plans inhibit performance in the field, and decisions are too rarely timely, disciplined, or supported by adequate problem analyses.
- Disunity of effort predominates at a cost of lost American lives, resources, and power.[3]

To take one example, inadequate interagency cooperation created critical vulnerabilities before the impending September 11, 2001 (9/11) debacle. In 2000, a Federal Bureau of Investigation (FBI) agent investigating the bombing of the USS *Cole* discovered a connection to al-Qaeda by way of a terrorist organizer named Khallad and a meeting of operatives in Malaysia. Multiple requests to the Central Intelligence Agency (CIA) for more information on Khallad by the agent were denied. Had this information been forthcoming, the agent would have learned that two meeting attendees were indeed al-Qaeda operatives living in the United States. Instead, our national security system prevented information critical to America's safety from reaching the people who needed it most. As a direct result, more than 2,000 people lost their lives on American soil.[4]

And these problems still persist! Recent congressional testimony on the Provincial Reconstruction Teams (PRTs) in Afghanistan — a key institution for winning this vital conflict — notes that:

> [T]he mission has not been clearly defined. There is a lack of unity of command resulting in a lack of unity of effect. Funding is not consolidated . . . and funding streams are extremely confusing. Selection, skill sets . . . and training of PRT personnel continue to be problematic. Metrics do not exist for determining if PRTs are succeeding.[5]

There are five overarching explanations for the failures of the 1947 system as it operates today. First, gross systemic imbalance impedes policy integration because autonomous government entities are coupled with weak integration mechanisms. Second, the various national security elements are not managed as a cohesive system but are addressed as discrete components. Third, lower levels of government lack strong integration tools, forcing management responsibilities onto an overburdened White House. Fourth, the current security apparatus lacks an effective system for developing strategies that connect available resources, desired end states, and implementation procedures. Fifth, as currently organized, Congress is not equipped to provide a comprehensive assessment of U.S. national security missions; rather, it narrowly oversees individual policies and the discrete components of the system.

Problem #1: Autonomous Agencies Resist a Whole of Government Approach to Missions.

The negative effects of interagency fratricide are readily apparent. Bureaucratic decisionmaking mechanisms fail to produce timely unified strategic guidance. Individual agencies typically lack the ability to compel action, while interdepartmental authorities are often ambiguous. Institution-specific values prevail since a sense of interagency culture remains limited. Information sharing is not the norm. Communications predominately follow vertical channels. Disorganized, nonexistent, or otherwise flawed strategies result from these conditions.

Of course, agencies and departments wish to maintain their autonomy, but a successful national effort requires interagency cooperation in achieving solutions. While each individual organization occupies its own silo, vertically organized and largely separated from other government entities, U.S. national security problems are horizontal; they span departmental borders, requiring whole of government responses. Henry Kissinger once described the kind of strategy that results from this separation by capabilities: "It is as if in commissioning a painting, a patron would ask one artist to draw the face, another the body, another the hands, and still another the feet, simply because each artist is particularly good in one category."[6]

Although intelligence threats are aimed at the United States as a whole, most agencies conduct counterintelligence (CI) operations as discrete functions of their own agendas. Domestic and overseas CI threats are treated as separate jurisdictions, despite the fact that from the point of view of a foreign attacker, these targets are closely related. In fact, each federal department or agency that deals with sensitive material has its own in-house CI office, with little coordination between them. Even with the establishment of a National Counterintelligence Executive (NCIX) to create and enforce a common counterintelligence doctrine, separate jurisdictions for CI activities and reluctance to share personnel have weakened the ability of the NCIX to affect tactical operations. In turn, frustrations with an ineffectual NCIX simply lead the federal agencies to reinforce their own separate CI offices.[7]

Problem #2: Components of National Security Are Not Managed as a System.

The U.S. national security system is arguably the largest organizational decisionmaking system in the world.[8] The national security agencies can bring a wealth of experience, vision, and tools to bear on security challenges, but more often than not, the mechanisms to integrate the various dimensions of national security policy and to translate that policy into integrated programs and actions are extremely weak, if they exist at all. Components of the system are dispersed throughout the federal government, state and local entities, in overseas missions, and within the private sector. Yet, no overarching strategy connects the various parts. The Departments of Homeland Security (DHS) and Justice compete over terrorism prevention and response; Departments of Energy and DHS compete over preparing cities against nuclear or radiological attack as well as over which agency should have primary responsibility to safeguard U.S. bioterrorism research facilities from rogue employees. This kind of competition is a symptom of weak or failed integration. Without unified strategic direction, the system lacks unity of purpose.

The former National Security Council and Homeland Security Council staffs, now collectively known as the National Security Staff, are the President's main instruments of integration. Unfortunately, collectively they are too limited in size and authority to overcome these problems. Weak integrating mechanisms such as these are dominated by strong functional organizations that control policy implementation.

Although the National Security Advisor (NSA) is institutionally positioned to promote interagency collaboration and efficient policy implementation, the incumbent often lacks the authority to achieve these ends since mechanisms for delegating presidential authority are also inadequate. Despite the importance of mid-level officials below the NSC level in addressing urgent national security decisions, such interagency authorities are similarly anemic. As a result, key actors work around established interagency processes to execute policy.

Direct and sustained presidential engagement can sometimes overcome these problems and achieve successful policy development, implementation, and outcomes. At the same time, the national security system's excessive reliance on presidential leadership reflects and exacerbates the weak nature of existing interagency mechanisms. In the absence of direct and constant presidential intervention, the development and implementation of integrated national security strategies become problematic as policy coherence suffers under the weight of bureaucratic infighting.

This stalemate creates excessive veto opportunities. It encourages a search for consensus decisions based on the least common denominator, typically yielding policies that favor slow, incremental, and middle-of-the road courses of action. The Bay of Pigs fiasco is a telling example. The CIA's original "Trinidad Plan" for the Cuban operation, developed under President Eisenhower, was reviewed and approved, albeit unenthusiastically, by a committee of the Joint Chiefs of Staff (JCS). President Kennedy's initial hesitance to support the proposal was further reinforced by Secretary of State Dean Rusk, who thought that the spectacular operation could not successfully conceal U.S. involvement. Pursuant to Kennedy's guidelines, the CIA quickly reorganized the attack. The Agency selected the Bay of Pigs as the new landing site and formulated what became known as Operation ZAPATA. Operation ZAPATA was considered by the CIA and JCS to be less optimal than the Trinidad Plan, though this judgment was unknown to the President at the time. Strategic changes continued even once the operation was underway in an effort to meet various agency concerns. Thus, what began as a poorly planned attack progressed to a poorly integrated ad hoc invasion.

Frustrated with the impediments to developing integrated strategies, policymakers often bypass established decisionmaking mechanisms and employ informal structures and processes. Excluding key actors from decisionmaking occurred during the Iran-Contra affair, the Iraq war, and other crises, contributing to suboptimal policy choices. The widespread use of informal structures comes at the expense of interagency accountability and integration. Without delineated policy processes, leadership is difficult.

Problem #3: An Overburdened White House Is Forced to Centralize Issue Management.

The paucity of effective policy integration processes forces an overburdened White House to manage many national security efforts. According to one calculation, more than 29 agencies or special groups report directly to the President.[9] Such an over-centralized leadership structure does not allow for effective integration. The President does not have the time to become intimately involved in the management of multiple agencies. Yet, he or she is ultimately responsible for making decisions based on their findings.

The nature of the presidential office and reliance on political appointees discourages a whole of government approach. In this system, even the President's personally appointed cabinet members more effectively represent their specific departmental interests than the President's agenda. The commander in chief often favors the counsel of close advisors over that of cabinet officials. This mistrust causes many decisions to be made in the Oval Office without a more inclusive perspective.

In an effort to delegate authority, past Presidents have turned to one of two ineffective methods of integrated policy administration: appointing a lead agency or a lead individual. The lead agency approach generally results in other agencies providing insufficient support for common efforts. Typically, lead agency really means sole agency as no one will follow the lead if its directions substantially affect their organizational equities. Former NSA Zbigniew Brzezinski observed that:

Integration is needed, but this cannot be achieved from a departmental vantage point. No self-respecting Secretary of Defense will willingly agree to have his contribution, along with those of other agencies, integrated for presidential decision by another departmental secretary — notably, the Secretary of State. And no self-respecting Secretary of State will accept integration by a Defense Secretary. It has to be done by someone close to the president, and perceived as such by all the principals.[10]

Likewise, a lead individual ends up depending on his or her relationship with the President and influence with the White House. A senior participant said that one reason for this is, "It's very hard to have any player be both a player and the referee. The assistant secretary of state comes to the meeting to chair it and to represent the State Department. This puts him in an extremely difficult position, particularly when other agencies have equal or greater equities."[11] A lead individual is sometimes called a czar. A Washington saying about czars observes, "The barons ignore them, and eventually the peasants kill them."[12]

Neither of these faulty solutions has de facto or de jure authority to command agencies or departments. The result tends to be a breakdown in communication and a lack of concerted effort.

Problem #4: Resources Are Not Aligned with Strategic Objectives.

The allocation of resources is a good litmus test for effective leadership management. Budgeting for national security activities is integrated with strategy, assessment, planning, policy guidance, and evaluation only when leaders demand that this connection prevails. All too often, strategies and policies are developed without consideration of available resources. Leaders frequently pursue strategies without resources adequate to implement them effectively. This practice wastes time and money by misleading leaders about the capabilities at their disposal.

A related problem is that budget processes and human resource systems are agency focused. The national security system provides resources for national security functions, not national missions. As a result, resource allocation processes do not provide the full range of required capabilities. They also do not permit the system to surge in response to emergencies, or allow sufficient resource flexibility in response to changing priorities. Resources cannot simply migrate between departments when needed.

In most cases, budgets are developed and appropriated along departmental lines. Resources are then received and disbursed through departmental capabilities. In many cases, interagency centers and activities are under-resourced due to these department-focused allocation systems, which tend to favor core agency needs and priorities. Even when there is a central organization or individual in charge of coordinating interagency efforts, that leader often has little control over resources. Instead, his role in securing financial support for a mission is reduced to encouraging individual agencies to pick up the costs. Small bureaucratic bodies (such as the National Counterintelligence Executive in its early years) face challenges recruiting the best and the brightest people despite the importance of their missions since career paths within such groups—especially opportunities for advancement—are naturally limited. In addition, civilian agencies that are not traditionally associated with overseas activities tend to have difficulty contributing personnel to such missions.

Furthermore, the individual departments are rarely, if ever, offered incentives for funding interagency activities, resulting in limited integrated efforts. An agency will frequently respond to another agency's request for a concerted effort by asking who will finance the joint work. An article in the *Foreign Service Journal* notes that "establishing the teams in Iraq has been challenging, in part because of high-level wrangling between State and the Defense Department over who would provide security, support, and funding. No memorandum of understanding was in place to delineate each agency's responsibilities."[13] In this manner, focus is shifted from planning and execution and towards questions of financial responsibility. This approach is counterproductive to the process of establishing an integrated national security system.

When President Clinton wanted to send police to restore order in Haiti in 1994, several members of the NSC met to coordinate a response to the situation. The Department of Justice member said his department lacked money. Other members pointed out that their departments lacked trained police. Ultimately, the Army was the only capable, well-funded agency willing to provide personnel and resources. The Army sent a full division and a contingent of Special Forces, even though they were ill-suited for police work. The United Nations (UN), which eventually took control of the mission, requested that the Special Forces remain in Haiti, but the Army withdrew them as quickly as possible.

Problem #5: Congress Cannot Provide a Whole of Government Approach Due to a Focus on the Parts.

As presently organized, Congress oversees each agency and program individually, with committees directly corresponding to the structure of the executive branch agencies. No committee has oversight jurisdiction over the whole national security system, its core missions, or interagency operations. Instead, the committees for defense, foreign policy, and other executive branch agencies strictly divide the subject matter pie, leaving a large gap in oversight of interagency operations. In the case of China policy during the Clinton administration, Chinese trade, diplomatic, defense, and human rights issues were each debated in separate committees, with no congressional committee devoted to overseeing whether each of these policies fit into a cohesive strategy.

The ways in which the legislative branch allocates funds and conducts oversight reinforce existing systemic deficiencies, making improvements in performance more difficult. The foreign policy agencies fail to receive current congressional guidance, revised authorities, and timely funding. Restrictions on allocating or shifting funds frequently create problems. In 1993, a 4-month delay in obtaining congressional approval for a police training program in Somalia led to program failure since U.S. trainers were already slated to be withdrawn. On a larger scale, earmarking limitations in 1996 constrained U.S. Agency for International Development's (USAID) ability to respond proactively to the signing of a peace agreement between the government of the Philippines and the Moro National Liberation Front.

THE WAY AHEAD

How to successfully restructure the U.S. national security system to address these weaknesses? First, it is imperative to integrate more effectively the elements of American power through a whole of government approach. Second, the United States will need to create and empower superior leadership throughout the national security structure. These steps are inseparable. Superior leaders are needed to achieve the improved system integration as well as to accomplish other necessary reforms.

The project report *Forging a New Shield* describes how a successful national security system depends on the integration of all U.S. Government entities. Achieving such unity requires strong leadership at all levels of government, not just at the presidential level. A stable and effective national security system relies on interagency cooperation in planning, strategy, and implementation. Achieving enduring success requires a comprehensive strategy that draws together all the resources of the U.S. Government and that has enough public support to endure from election to election and from administration to administration.

Achieving Integration Through a Whole of Government Approach.

President Barack Obama began this process of integration on May 26, 2009, when he merged the Homeland Security Council and National Security Council staffs into a single National Security Staff. In line with a PNSR recommendation, the President stated: "Homeland Security is indistinguishable from National Security — conceptually, and functionally, they should be thought of together, rather than separately."[14]

PNSR advises that NSC members should not be prescribed statutorily. Rather, the President should have the flexibility to fashion the appropriate team for the situation at hand. While a core set of personnel should remain to ensure continuity, participation in each meeting should be discretionary, allowing members to choose the meetings that demand their particular expertise. In this way, the President can hold joint meetings among experts in different fields to discuss — for example, international security, economic security, and homeland security issues — while still ensuring that council members uninvolved in a particular issue do not attend unnecessarily. During the confirmation process for NSC principals, senators should ensure that nominees are dedicated to working as a part of a highly collaborative system and fully committed to supporting missions at the national level. This team will establish the vision which the rest of the national security system should seek to implement.

The missions formulated by the President and NSC must be executed in a similar spirit of collaboration. The goal should be to unify the efforts of each component of the national security system and decentralize the management of issues. The process must begin by shifting away from departmental-specific groups towards interagency panels or teams. Teams should be created to focus on presidential priority concerns. Some of the best examples of successful interagency teams are the two Joint Interagency Task Forces involved in counternarcotics. According to Scott Feil, these interagency task forces "bring together domestic and foreign policy agencies and departments with various authorities, thus providing effective counter-drug operations based on core competencies, authorities, and resources of the respective agencies."[15]

Empowering Leaders.

National security success depends on establishing a good structure and process, but having superior human capital is even more important. Yet, few if any incentives currently exist for men and women to serve on interagency teams. Potential new incentives to ensure collaboration could include expanded joint or combined agency training, more opportunities for professional education in the entire range of U.S. national security activities, and rotations and exchanges between agencies.

Web-based collaboration sites, meetings, and town hall events could help facilitate these incentives and interagency activities. These activities could be coordinated by the executive secretary of the NSC, advised by a Human Capital Advisory Board. A cadre of National Security Executives (NSEs) appointed by the President would have formal authority over interagency teams. The NSEs should be highly respected individuals who are experts in their specialty areas and known for their leadership abilities. A National Security Professional Corps should be created to recruit and retain qualified personnel.

Promotion incentives must also be established to encourage employees within the system to adopt a whole of government mindset. Individuals who have served in interagency roles or rotated through multiple agencies or departments should be granted significant credit during promotion evaluations. In addition, an interagency assignment should be a prerequisite for anyone wishing to be promoted to a senior rank.

The existing National Security Education Consortium (established by Executive Order 13434) should serve as the foundation for developing a comprehensive professional education and training program. This program will focus on nurturing skills and a positive culture throughout the system.

Although many practitioners agree with the problem analysis and recommendations put forth by PNSR, they question whether such comprehensive reforms are possible. The 9/11 Commission report noted, "Americans should not settle for incremental, ad hoc adjustments to a system designed generations ago for a world that no longer exists."[16] We at PNSR definitely agree!

The legislative and executive branches must respond to the new challenges that the 21st century presents to the national security system. In a world of increased globalization, unpredictable terrorist attacks, pandemics, and weapons of mass destruction, the United States cannot continue to rely on the system designed by lawmakers in 1947. Maintaining the old system in the face of a new environment is anachronistic and irresponsible. Reforming the system by removing impediments to better performance and eliminating recurring problems with due attention to their causes is long overdue. Achieving strong national security leadership through a holistic approach is crucial for addressing the weaknesses of the current system. PNSR is eager to support the Obama administration, Congress, the Strategic Studies Institute of the U.S. Army War College, and others seeking to ensure Americans' security in the 21st century.

ENDNOTES - CHAPTER 2

1. George B. Shaw, Famous Quotes and Authors, available from *www.famousquotesandauthors.com/authors/george_bernard_shaw_quotes.html.*

2. Bradley H. Patterson, *To Serve the President: Continuity and Innovation in the White House Staff,* Washington, DC: Brookings Institution Press, 2008, p. 38.

3. For the specific cases documenting these conclusions, see Richard Weitz, ed., *Project on National Security Reform: Case Studies,* Vol. 1, Washington, DC: Project on National Security Reform, 2008, available from *www.pnsr.org/data/files/pnsr%20case%20studies%20vol.%201.pdf.*

4. James R. Locher III, "The Most Important Thing: Legislative Reform of the National Security System," *Military Review,* May-June, 2008, available from *www.pnsr.org/data/images/military_review_article.pdf.*

5. *Forging a New Shield,* Washington, DC: Project on National Security Reform, 2008, p. 151, available from *www.pnsr.org/data/files/pnsr%20forging%20a%20new%20shield.pdf.*

6. *Ibid.,* p. 155.

7. Michelle Van Cleave, "The NCIX and the National Counterintelligence Mission: What Has Worked, What Has Not, and Why," Richard Weitz, ed., *Project on National Security Reform: Case Studies,* Vol. 1, Washington, DC: Project on National Security Reform, 2008, pp. 59-130.

8. *Forging a New Shield,* p. 221.

9. *Ibid.,* p. vii.

10. *Ibid.,* p. 139

11. *Ibid.*

12. *Ibid.*

13. *Ibid.*, p. 247.

14. "Organizing for Homeland Security and Counterter-rorism," Presidential Study Directive-1, The White House, February 23, 2009, available from *www.fas.org/irp/offdocs/psd/psd-1.pdf*.

15. Scott R. Feil, "The Failure of Incrementalism: Interagency Coordination Challenges and Responses," Joseph R. Cerami and Jay W. Boggs, eds., *The Interagency and Counterinsurgency Warfare: Stability, Security, Transition, and Reconstruction Roles*, Carlisle, PA: Strategic Studies Institute, U.S. Army War College, 2007, pp. 308-310.

16. *The 9/11 Commission Report*, Washington, DC: U.S. Government Printing Office, July 22, 2004, p. 399.

CHAPTER 3

LEADERSHIP AS PRACTICAL ETHICS

Joel H. Rosenthal

What does one need to know to be a leader in the field of public policy? I want to argue for the centrality of ethics as a basic component of leadership training for anyone pursuing a career in public and international affairs.

If you are a student, please take a moment to ask yourself what you have learned about ethics in your time in the classroom. If you are a teacher or administrator, consider what your curriculum covers in this regard. We know that medical students engage medical ethics, law students study legal ethics, business students take on business ethics, military officers study military ethics, and so on. So let's ask ourselves, what should students and aspiring leaders in public affairs know about ethics to be considered professionals competent to practice?

By ethics, I do not mean simply compliance with law. Compliance is, of course, an essential part of ethics. But it is only a beginning. Compliance is a floor, a minimum upon which to build. Many actions in government, business, or private life comply with the law but are not optimal from an ethical perspective. Examples are all around us. British members of parliament may not have broken laws when they used expense accounts to bill taxpayers for lifestyle enhancements such as moat cleaning, the upkeep of expensive second homes, or the rental of adult movies. But surely this kind of behavior was wrong. In more serious policy matters, it may well be that most of our major banks and financial institutions were in full compliance with the law when it came to the management of credit default swaps and derivative trading. Yet something went very wrong in the area of risk and responsibility. There are many things we can do and still be in compliance with law — but some of them are wrong. Ethical reasoning helps us make these distinctions.

The discipline of ethics begins with Socrates' question: How should one live? Ethics is about choice. What values guide us? What standards do we use? What principles are at stake, and how do we choose between them? An ethical approach to a problem will inquire about ends (goals) and means (the instruments we use to achieve these goals), and the relationship between the two.

Ethical reasoning is the process of raising awareness of moral claims and applying principles to arising circumstances. Ethical reasoning implies an interrogation of the moral claims that surround us rather than a mere listing of dos and don'ts. In a word, ethical inquiry is proactive rather than passive.

The philosopher Simon Blackburn writes that ethics takes as its starting point that "human beings are ethical animals . . . we grade and evaluate, and compare and admire, and claim and justify. . . . Events endlessly adjust our sense of responsibility, our guilt and our shame, and our sense of our own worth and that of others." [1]

According to Blackburn, ethical inquiry is normative in the sense that it suggests "norms." Norms are what we consider "expected and required" behavior. We all experience functional norms. For example, in the United States, drivers stay on the right-hand side of the road; in the United Kingdom (UK), drivers keep to the left. But we also experience moral norms. A moral norm would consist of an expectation such as non-discrimination in the workplace or the requirement to respect the needs of the most vulnerable members of society (e.g. children, elderly, and the infirm). Moral norms are aspirational and prescriptive rather than functional and descriptive — they paint the "ought" rather than the "is." It is this type of norm that I want to focus on in this chapter.

A cautionary note is necessary here. Norms, expectations, and ethical claims depend deeply on context. No single normative theory or formula will suffice across different types of examples. One of the great ethicists of recent memory, Isaiah Berlin, famously gave up his Oxford chair in normative theory, so the story goes, because he felt he had no single normative theory to purvey. Berlin did not pretend to offer a grand theory that would meet the test of the many different types of cases he was concerned with.[2]

Berlin's work reminds us that normative inquiry is a nonperfectionist art. The first lesson of ethics is that values overlap and conflict. The single-minded pursuit of any particular virtue can subvert a competing virtue. So as we often see, freedom can conflict with order, justice with mercy, and truth with loyalty. In international affairs, peace may be our goal, but we cannot ignore the need to confront aggression. Some may chant "no more war." These same people may also chant "never again genocide." Sometimes, tragically and unavoidably, force is needed to prevent harm. Here, and in countless similar examples, we see norms clashing. Berlin lets us know that these clashes happen more often than not.

ETHICS IN THREE DIMENSIONS

Despite our lack of a single theory or formula, Berlin and others do offer a framework for ethical reasoning. Inspired by Berlin and other pragmatists, I think of this framework as ethics in three dimensions. The first dimension focuses on the decisionmaker — the actor or the agent who makes a choice. We can and should evaluate the acts of individuals, be they presidents, ministers, official representatives, chief executive officers (CEOs), community leaders, advocates, employees, consumers, or citizens. Each has a role as an ethically autonomous actor.

At first glance, the idea of the autonomous actor seems simple and straightforward. However, we should bear in mind that identity is fluid, not static. Most individuals have multiple identities. For example, a single individual could say: I am British. I am a Muslim. I am a woman. I am a professor. I am a feminist. Clearly, many sets of values make up a composite yet single-actor identity in such an example. Each element of one's identity plays an important role in determining which of one's many values and allegiances may have priority. Claims of national loyalty, religious obligation, professional codes of conduct, and solidarity around an issue of social justice and concern might all come into play. This is the way life is actually lived, isn't it?[3]

In addition to single actors, a discussion of moral agents must also consider the identity, values, and acts of collective actors such as states, corporations, nongovernmental organizations (NGOs), and international organizations. One of the most important trends of our time is the growing power of nonstate actors — especially multinational corporations. Wal-

Mart, Microsoft, and other companies of this size and scope rival the capacities of many states in terms of their economic, political, and social reach. It is therefore both necessary and proper to ask and answer questions relating to the moral choices of corporate entities. All are moral agents.

The second dimension of ethics has to do with the systems, social arrangements, and conditions that define our range of choices. In short, we need to examine the "rules of the game" by which we live and make decisions. We all live within sets of norms and expectations—some more fair and just than others. Perhaps the best way to illustrate this dimension is to examine examples of when "rational" choices within a set of arrangements yield "bad" or less-than-desirable results. In other words, in some systems, when one does the "right thing" within the system, the net result is suboptimal.

Consider consumer behavior when shopping for clothes. It usually makes sense to buy the least expensive shirt available when quality between competing options is equal. But because of the supply chain of the global economy, that shirt may be produced in a sweatshop that runs on child labor. Buying the least expensive shirt of equal quality might be rational according to market design—yet the result might be ethically troubling.

This problem exists on many levels of policy and institutional design. For example, consider the nuclear weapons doctrine of mutual assured destruction (MAD). The entire strategic framework is based on the idea of reciprocal threat. Within this system, to ensure stability, the most rational thing to do is to make an immoral threat (and be prepared to carry it out).

Clearly, there is something deeply troubling about MAD. It would seem to me to be a worthy goal to try to create frameworks and policies where the rational thing to do would be more benign than to make a threat of MAD. In brief, then, this second dimension calls attention to the fact that we live within institutions, systems, and social arrangements of human design. The rules, norms, and conditions of these arrangements should be subject to ethical evaluation.

The third dimension of ethics is the assertion that we often have the opportunity to improve our situation—to do better. One way to think of this is to consider a standard ethics scenario like this: My mother is sick. I cannot afford medicine. So I steal the medicine from a pharmacy whose managers will not even notice that it is gone. Is stealing the medicine in this circumstance the right thing or the wrong thing to do? We can discuss this case in terms of my decision as a moral agent—whether I am a thief and villain, a rescuer and a hero, or both. Ethical questions are frequently raised as dilemmas such as this one. In many situations, there is a genuine need to choose between two competing and compelling claims, and ethical reasoning can help to sort these out. But we can also expand the inquiry to ask a broader question beyond the narrow question of whether to steal or not to steal. We can also ask: What kind of community denies medicine to sick people who cannot afford it? Is there something unfair or unethical about this system?

To further illustrate this third dimension, it is useful to note the distinction that Andrew Carnegie drew between charity and philanthropy.[4] Charity, according to Carnegie, is the duty to attend to immediate and acute human suffering. Charity translates to feeding the hungry, tending to the sick and destitute, providing relief to victims of natural and man-made disasters, and giving shelter to the homeless. Philanthropy is something different—it is an endeavor that reaches above and beyond the imperatives of charity. Philanthropy explores new ways of living, new ideas, and new institutions to improve society.

While this may sound abstract, Carnegie's philanthropy was specific and practical. He addressed the societal-level problem of education by suggesting and then providing the infrastructure for two institutions we now take for granted: the public library and the teacher pension system. Carnegie believed that every person should have access to knowledge. Universal literacy and educational opportunity would be possible by supporting a free public library system which he began to do all across the United States, and to a much lesser extent, the UK (his place of birth). In his lifetime, Carnegie provided funds to build more than 2,500 public library buildings.

Carnegie's library venture was an extraordinary feat totaling $41 million dollars, easily several billion in today's dollars. Yet, tellingly, he asked municipal leaders to be partners in the enterprise by providing the books and the funds for upkeep. Carnegie would build the buildings, but communities would be responsible for whatever happened next. Carnegie thought that if these institutions had real value, communities would invest in them rather than merely accept them passively as gifts. Similarly, when he decided to provide the funds to build Carnegie Hall in New York City, he built the structure in all its grandeur, but he did not leave an endowment for maintenance. He believed that if the music hall had genuine value, its patrons—those who benefitted from it—would contribute to its upkeep.

Carnegie also created the first teacher pension institution—now known as TIAA-CREF—to help professionalize the vocation of teaching. If teachers were undervalued, as some surmised, then here was an institution that would contribute to improvement of the educational system by supporting teachers. The idea was simple, but its ramifications were profound. With proper pay and retirement benefits enabled by the new pension system, teaching would become a fully modern profession.

Similarly, when it came to politics, Carnegie believed that new institutions could improve public policy. Specifically, as an advocate for the peaceful resolution of international conflicts and disputes, Carnegie supported the mediation and arbitration movement that grew out of Geneva in the mid-19th century. Again, the idea was elegant in its simplicity and grandeur. Just as we have legal mechanisms to arbitrate disputes in domestic society, so too can we have mechanisms in international society for the same purpose. The concept of international law and organization was gaining momentum at the beginning of the 20th century—the movement merely needed new institutions to give it shape and force. In this spirit, Carnegie financed the building of the Peace Palace at The Hague in the Netherlands, supported the establishment of the International Court of Justice, and lobbied for the establishment of the League of Nations. Carnegie devoted much of his philanthropy—and his personal energy—to promoting these new institutions and the ideas behind them.

So then the third dimension of ethics expands the range of choices we have in front of us. It is about creating new possibilities. I like to picture this idea in its cartoon form. For me, it is comes to life in the character of Bugs Bunny. The narrative is familiar. Our hero gets into trouble and runs away from a threatening pursuer. But he is eventually backed into a corner. There is no escape. What does he do? He reaches into his pocket and miraculously pulls out a pen or marker. He then proceeds to draw a picture of a window on the blank wall. The image of the window becomes real. Then he climbs out. Sometimes we do face genuine dilemmas—and the lines we draw on the wall remain lines. But other times we can and should imagine better options.

LEADERSHIP AS PRACTICAL ETHICS

How then, do we connect this understanding of the three dimensions of ethics to leadership? Leadership is as vast a topic as ethics, so let us begin with some simple concepts. In his new book, *George Washington on Leadership*, Richard Brookhiser describes leadership as "knowing yourself, knowing where you want to go, and then taking others to that new place."[5] There are many ways to lead; there are many styles and countless examples to study. One way to focus our analysis is to examine in detail the ends/means/consequences equation as Brookhiser suggests. This leads to three questions: What is the goal? What means will we use to get there? And what types of trade-offs and compromises must be made along the way?

Brookhiser's observations remind me of one of my favorite undergraduate lectures on American political history. The lecture was delivered by Professor Frank Freidel, a biographer of Franklin Roosevelt (FDR). His topic was FDR's leadership style. Professor Freidel drew a simple X at the top/center of the blackboard. He then drew a zig-zagging line from the bottom of the blackboard up to the top. He explained that Roosevelt thought of himself as a sailor heading upwind. The destination was certain—the fixed point represented by the X. Each zig-zag represented a tack back-and-forth needed to approach the goal.

As any sailor knows, when in a sail boat, you cannot head directly into the wind. If you try to sail straight into the wind, the sails flap around uselessly, the boat stalls, and you are unable to move forward. So like any experienced helmsman, Roosevelt understood the need to tack back and forth. Each tack could mean an uncertain and uneasy compromise. Sometimes he would have to tack horizontally just to maintain his previous gains. Yet each compromise was necessary to maintain way against the headwinds that would mercilessly beat him back or blow him off course.

If we accept leadership as goal-driven and compromise-ridden, then we see that ethics should not be merely peripheral to any public policy curriculum or program of leadership development. Ethics is neither a luxury nor a hurdle to be cleared. It is intrinsic to decisionmaking and leadership itself.

In his book, *Ethics as Practice*, Hugh LaFollette explains that ethics, like medicine, is a practical art.[6] Just as we study medicine not only to learn about the body and its functions, but to make us better by promoting good health, so too we study ethics not merely for philosophical enlightenment, but to improve the quality of our lives. Ethics helps us to understand what we truly value and how to connect this with the practice of our daily lives, our individual choices, and the policies of the institutions of which we are a part.

Pragmatists, like pluralists, argue that the moral and the practical are inextricably linked. Let me give you an example drawn from the history of my institution, the Carnegie Council, which was founded in

58

1914 by Andrew Carnegie as one of his peace endowments. Its purpose then, as it is now, is to serve as an educational resource—a center for ideas and action—for leaders in the academic and policy communities. Writing in 1937 about the future of the peace movement, my predecessor as leader of the council, Henry Atkinson, made this point:

> The reason for the long list of failures [of the peace movement] is that the idealism of the idealist is seldom put into practice. The eminent Boston physician Dr. Richardson Cabot, speaking of ethics, said, "Most of what used to be called goodness has rightly fallen into disrepute because it is inefficient. As I see it, ethical diagnosis, like physical diagnosis, has a practical end."[7]

In citing Dr. Cabot, Atkinson understood that ethics is intrinsic to what we do, not extrinsic. No project is sustainable if it is built on faulty assumptions. Nothing good, and certainly nothing great, can be built upon ignorance, misperception, or misplaced idealism. A moral commitment without a sense of realism, a sense of how things actually work, is a recipe for disaster. Also, any practical scheme without a sense of the values that must support it is equally doomed.

Ethics and leadership are therefore best understood as a realist endeavor. Realists focus on power and interests as the key elements of human behavior. The Athenian generals in Thucydides' great history, *The Peloponnesian War*, are often quoted as the authority on this point: "The strong do what they will and the weak do what they must." We neglect this basic insight about power at our own peril.

Yet with this point made, sophisticated realists will also understand that while the drive for power and the maximizing of interests explains much, the concept of interest is often more than just the accumulation and exertion of power. Interests are not always obvious. They can be complex, diverse, and hard to isolate. There are also obvious limits to power. Thucydides and his realist disciples, Nicollo Machiavelli and Thomas Hobbes, were quick to recognize that some outcomes cannot be achieved by brute force alone, and that the exertion of power always raises the specters of overreach and corruption. In understanding the complexities of power, realists are perhaps the best proponents of the concept of enlightened self-interest. Simply put, enlightened self-interest begins with our own needs, yet it also takes into account the needs and interests of others.

Any good realist will tell you that taking into account the interests of others is not altruism. Rather, it is realism at its best. In her book, *Moral Clarity*, Susan Neiman writes: "Hobbes . . . imagines a state of nature whose wild hordes are just rational enough to stop their rush toward doomsday by agreeing to obey any sovereign who will prevent further war."[8] Neiman reminds us through the example of Hobbes that even in the darkest, crudest version of the war of all against all, some notion of rationality prevails. Limits are recognized. Cooperation becomes possible by yielding to the overarching power of the Leviathan. In the Hobbesian state of nature, conflict has its limits and cooperation around enlightened self-interest, albeit in a limited form, is a strategy for survival.

Recent literature in evolutionary biology and neuroscience investigates the notion that enlightened self-interest may be hard-wired as a matter of natural selection and the instinct to survive. Robert Wright's book, *Non-Zero: The Logic of Human Destiny*, explores the idea that human history and interaction can be best explained by observing non-zero sum, win-win, cooperative arrangements rather than zero-sum, winner-take-all competitions. He writes:

> In zero-sum games, the fortunes of the players are inversely related. In tennis, in chess, in boxing, one contestant's gain is another's loss. In non-zero games, one player's gain needn't be bad news for the other(s). . . . You can capture history's basic trajectory by reference to a core pattern: New technologies arise that permit or encourage new, richer forms of non-zero-sum interaction; then (for intelligible reasons grounded ultimately in human nature) social structures evolve that realize this rich potential — that convert non-zero sum situations into positive sums.[9]

The result is a world of cooperative structures that benefit most of the people most of the time. Neuroscience is beginning to show us that the "will to power" may have a companion in "cooperation" as a biological mechanism to enhance prospects for survival.

The proper discernment of power and interests in a globalized and highly interdependent world is no small matter. It is the first requirement of leadership. The three dimensions of ethics we have just discussed provide a framework for this discernment. Once we have established our bearings, it is then necessary to articulate the core principles of our ethical concern. In my experience, there are three core principles that have universal resonance, even if interpretations of each differ widely according to time, place, and circumstance. These principles are: pluralism, rights, and fairness. Each principle provides a point of reference from which we can rehearse arguments with ourselves and others, and then make ethically informed decisions.

AN ETHICAL FRAMEWORK: THREE PRINCIPLES

Pluralism begins with appreciation for diversity while recognizing what is common in the human experience. A value such as self-interest and/or a moral sentiment such as honor or fairness will develop differently according to time, place, and circumstance. Yet there is something that binds us — and that "something" is the capacity to enter into a value system that is not our own.

Simon Blackburn, James Rachels, and other philosophers make this point by citing an example from Herodotus' *Histories* regarding funeral customs.[10] We know that in some societies the most common funeral custom is to bury the dead. In other societies, it is customary to cremate the dead as on a funeral pyre. In still others, the custom is to eat (!) the dead. Members of each society think that their custom is best, and that others are misguided or worse. The point here is not to say that one's own customs are always superior. Nor is the point the opposite: that all customs are relative and are purely matters of convenience. Rather, the point of this example is that there is a central truth — respect for the dead — that takes different forms in different circumstances.

Pluralism's first argument is with monism. Monists are purveyors of moral clarity, single-minded advocates of a truth as they see it. As such, monists adhere to familiar custom and dogma, the validity of which is based on faith and will remain beyond human reason and reach. Monists neglect the idea that our understanding of the truth may change over time, especially in light of new information and experience.

Monists will resist the idea that truths are many, not one, and that while we often agree on those verifiable observations we call facts, we often do not agree on their meaning. Enlightened realists remind us that humility is required in the face of conviction. Pluralists remind us that, ironically, the one thing we should agree upon is the possibility that we can be wrong. The realist and pluralist point of view does not resonate with monists, who are more comfortable in the waters of moral certainty.

We feel the full weight of pluralism when we view a great work of art or read a classic text. Through these encounters, we can understand the experiences and the value systems of others. We enter into another world and experience part of it as others did and do. Pluralism is a way to transcend the false dichotomy of monism and relativism. Monism holds that "only one set of values is true, all others are false." Relativism holds that "my values are mine, yours are yours, and if we clash, too bad, neither of us can claim to be right."[11] Most of us live in that interesting place in between—and this is the territory of the pluralist.

Reinhold Niebuhr has gained much attention recently as a favorite philosopher of the current President. This is no coincidence, as President Obama has charted a course that veers away from black and white, for us or against us, positions favored by President Bush. Columnist David Brooks captured the Niebuhrian spirit in 2002 in an *Atlantic* magazine article aptly titled "A Man on a Gray Horse."[12] The true moral course, according to Niebuhr, is often found in uneasy compromises and in shades of gray. The grayness of the horse is a reminder that we are far from pure; our history shows us that we sometimes act unjustly and impurely in our pursuit of justice. Niebuhr reminded us that even the "good war" ended with the atomic incineration of Hiroshima and Nagasaki. Brooks summarizes Niebuhr's point succinctly: "That in battling evil the United States would become intoxicated with illusions about its own goodness."[13]

In addition to the dangers of monism, pluralism also addresses the challenges of relativism. Relativism is the idea that every moral claim is just as good as any other, its well-worn mantra being, "One man's terrorist is another man's freedom fighter." One can try to make that argument, but it will not alter the fact that terrorism is the random slaying of innocent people. Another tired relativist argument is that norms are merely the reflection of the interests of the power actors who make the rules and stand to gain from their enforcement. While one may make this argument too, it will not alter the fact that freedom makes no sense without order, and that power must be deployed to ensure order. Power considerations cannot be wished away; and the actions of powerful actors should not be dismissed out of hand as morally suspect.

Pluralists hold firm against cynicism. They contend that it is both possible and necessary to sort out competing claims. Pluralists observe that every society has strongly developed codes of duty and restraint that promote some notion of human decency well-being. Part of what makes us human is our capacity to understand these norms, how they developed, and why — even if we strongly disagree with them. This open approach enhances the prospects for moral argument.

Isaiah Berlin gives us a classic example of how and why pluralism is not relativism. He writes:

> I find Nazi values detestable, but I can understand how, given enough misinformation, enough false

belief about reality, one could come to believe that
they are the only salvation. Of course they have to
be fought, by war if need be, but I do not regard the
Nazis as some people do, as literally pathological or
insane, only as wickedly wrong, totally misguided
about the facts, for example, in believing that some
beings are subhuman, that race is central, or that
Nordic races alone are truly creative, and so forth. I
see how, with enough false education, enough widespread illusion and error, men can, while remaining
men, believe this and commit the most unspeakable
crimes.[14]

Berlin's pluralism is not relativism because he first
empathizes, he seeks to understand the Nazi worldview on its own terms, and then he engages in moral
argument to refute it.

Another place to plant the flag against relativism
is on the high ground of "rights." By rights we mean
protections and entitlements in relation to duties and
responsibilities. Rights arguments are put forward
against arguments of utility. According to rights theo-
rists from Kant to Jefferson and beyond, there is something fundamental about being human (an inalienable
characteristic) that prohibits any person from being
treated as something merely useful, as a means to an
end.

The source of human rights is an unending debate. However, I am persuaded by pragmatists like
Judith Sklar, Amy Guttmann, and Michael Ignatieff
who argue that in the end, foundational arguments
may not really matter.[15] Empirical observation of the
need for human rights and the beneficient work that
human rights arguments do may be sufficient. After
all, the mass murders of the 20th century are proof of
the need for such protection. Think of the body counts
under the regimes of Adolph Hitler, Joseph Stalin, and
Mao Tse Tung. The facts of the genocides and gulags

in such recent memory should be sufficient to make the case that protections are needed. Duties to provide protection therefore follow.

Rights claims raise questions about assignment of responsibilities that are not always clear. One way to think about assignment of responsibilities is to consider rights claims in terms of perfect and imperfect obligations. Perfect obligations are specific and direct. For example, we have the perfect obligation not to torture. Imperfect obligations are more general, less specific, and inexactly targeted. So in the case of torture, there is the requirement "to consider the ways and means through which torture can be prevented."[16]

Or perhaps for a better illustration of the distinction between perfect and imperfect duties, consider the infamous case of Kitty Genovese. Kitty Genovese was a 28-year-old woman who lived in Kew Gardens, Queens, New York, in 1964. One night on her way home, she was stabbed several times by an unknown assailant and left to die. Her case became widely known because it was alleged that 38 people passed her by as she lay dying in the street, and no one helped her. Presumably, each of the 38 passers-by thought someone else would help, or they did not want to get involved. Whatever the precise details, this scenario helps to elucidate the point about perfect and imperfect duties. We all share the basic duty not to harm. However, we also share the basic duty to disallow the conditions of harm, and that when harm is done, to mitigate the effects of it. To echo a previous point, the exercise of imperfect duty is far from altruism. It is in our enlightened self-interest to live in a community where people are not left to die in the streets.

In looking at public policy today, we see several obvious cases where both our direct and indirect participation in the mitigation of harms is inevitable. As participants in the global economy, the global environment, and global security, we act both directly as agents and indirectly as bystanders. When we consume and travel, we engage in a system that provides benefits and places burdens. There is really no place to hide. As implicated agents in these social arrangements, our actions will be judged accordingly.

The third principle to consider is fairness. Ideas about fairness are highly subjective and heavily influenced by circumstances. As I have written elsewhere with my coauthor Ethan Kapstein, one of the most useful models for illustrating fairness considerations is the Ultimatum Game (UG).[17] In the game, two players have the opportunity to divide a pot of money. A Proposer (P) makes an offer to a Respondent (R) over how a pot of money should be divided. R can either accept P's offer — in which case the money is divided as P proposed — or R can reject the offer, in which case both players walk away with nothing.

The classic rational actor model of behavior predicts that, in such cases, the split might be something along the lines of 99:1; that is, P would offer R one unit while keeping 99 for himself. Since we can usually count on profit-maximizing behavior, this division makes both parties better off if unequal; there is no rational reason for R to reject it since R would receive nothing. Maximization strategies therefore lead to unequal divisions of a given pie.

But behavioral economists, repeating the UG in a variety of countries and under a variety of conditions, have observed a puzzling result. When Rs are offered an amount they consider to be unfair they reject it — they would prefer nothing to something. Indeed, realizing that unfair offers are likely to be rejected, Ps routinely offer about one-half the pot at the outset, and when asked why they do so they normally answer that "this seems fair."

Researchers have drawn several significant findings from the UG, all of which are relevant to the study of moral considerations in world politics. First, Ps adopt moral reasoning or other-regarding behavior out of their self-interest. Ps who do not care about what others think must nonetheless fear rejection of an unfair offer and the absence of any payoff whatsoever. The adoption of "fairness considerations" is therefore efficiency enhancing to the extent that it leads to an agreement and thus an increase in welfare for both of the agents.[18]

Second, P's concern with achieving an equitable or fair result arises in part from *uncertainty* about how R will respond to P's offer. If P knows that R will willingly accept the greedy offer, P will be much more inclined to propose a lopsided division. Not knowing R's response beforehand, P offers the amount that intuitively seems to be fair (i.e., equal division).

Returning to our theme of enlightened self-interest, fairness and reciprocity suggest that what is good for you often turns out to be what is good for others involved. This is the nature of complex problems and decisions. Taken to the global level, individual interests must be seen in terms of complex interdependence, international norms, and global responsibilities.

LEADERSHIP FOR REALISTS

While I hope these remarks have given you positive ideas about leadership, I also hope they have not promised too much. It is important to close with a sense of realism that reminds us of the limits of human achievement and the dangers of assuming harmonious outcomes. Good intentions are never enough. Leaders must always attend to consequences. Moral imperatives often conflict. Leaders must make difficult and imperfect choices. The word "utopia" derives from a Greek term meaning "no place." Utopia does not exist. And as we all know from history, it has been the pursuit of utopia — of perfect societies and outcomes — that has led to the worst episodes in human history.

There is much truth in such commonplace sayings as "leadership is a foul weather job" and organizations "rot from the head down." Burdens placed on leaders force them to be visionaries and exemplars — and yet, they can never be perfect nor should they aspire to be. Ethics plays a central role in navigating through the ideal vision and the realities of daily life. Ethics is a process, a constant reflection on aspirations and compromises. It is incumbent upon leaders to establish their normative vision and to measure their behavior accordingly. What are my goals? What are my core values? And what trade-offs am I willing to make? These questions never go away.

Management gurus are quick to point out that if we are not trying to improve, then we are sure to get worse. Commitment to our highest aspirations, openness, and self-correction is the essence of ethics in leadership. By suggesting three dimensions as points of entry into ethical inquiry — our roles as moral agents, as participants in the institutions in which we live, and as the architects of new institutions that will define our future — I hope I have given you a sense of the practical importance of ethics. By suggesting the principles of pluralism, rights, and fairness as the ground on which to plant your flag, I hope I have prepared you somewhat for your journey toward principled leadership.

ENDNOTES - CHAPTER 3

1. Simon Blackburn, *Ethics: A Very Short Introduction*, Oxford, UK: Oxford University Press, 2000.

2. Ryan Patrick Hanley, "Berlin and History," George Crowder and Henry Hardy, eds., *The One and the Many*, New York: Prometheus Books, 2007, pp. 159-180.

3. Amartya Sen, *Identity and Violence*, New York: W. W. Norton, 2006.

4. David Nasaw, *Andrew Carnegie*, New York: Penguin Press, 2006.

5. Richard Brookhiser, *George Washington on Leadership*, New York: Basic Books, 2008.

6. Hugh LaFollette, *The Practice of Ethics*, Malden, MA: Blackwell Publishing, 2007.

7. Henry Atkinson, *Prelude to Peace*, New York: Harper & Brothers, 1937, p. 3.

8. Susan Nieman, *Moral Clarity: A Guide for Grown-Up Idealists*, Orlando, FL: Harcourt, 2008, p. 30.

9. Robert Wright, *Non-Zero: The Logic of Human Destiny*, New York: Pantheon Books, 2000, p. 5.

10. James Rachels, *The Elements of Moral Philosophy*, Fourth Ed., Boston: McGraw-Hill, 2003, pp. 16-17.

11. Isaiah Berlin, "The First and the Last," *New York Review of Books*, May 14, 1997, p. 11.

12. David Brooks, "A Man on a Gray Horse," *Atlantic*, September 2002, available from *www.theatlantic.com/magazine/archive/2002/09/a-man-on-a-gray-horse/2558/*.

13. Ibid.

14. Berlin, p. 10.

15. Judith Sklar, "The Liberalism of Fear," Nancy L. Rosenblum, ed., *Liberalism and the Moral Life*, Cambridge, MA.: Harvard University Press, 1989; and Michael Ignatieff and Amy Gutmann, *Human Rights as Politics and Idolatry*, Princeton, NJ: Princeton University Press, 2001.

16. Amartya Sen, "Elements of a Theory of Human Rights," *Philosophy and Public Affairs*, 2004.

17. Ethan B. Kapstein and Joel H. Rosenthal, "Ethics in International Affairs: An Assessment," in *Ethics and International Affairs*, London, UK: Ashgate, 2009.

18. Ethan B. Kapstein, *Economic Justice in an Unfair World*, Princeton, NJ: Princeton University Press, 2006.

CHAPTER 4

TRANSFORMING INTELLIGENCE ANALYSIS: "THE TAIL THAT WAGS THE DOG"[1]

Richard H. Immerman[2]

Change is hard. We all know that. We also all know that organizational change is particularly hard, especially if that organization is large and its culture entrenched. This is true even if the organization is dynamic and successful, as is Microsoft. In such cases changes are normatively incremental and take years to produce the desired effect, or its approximation. Then there are organizations like General Motors (GM). "We have vastly underestimated how deeply ingrained are the organizational and cultural rigidities that hamper our ability to execute," conceded a GM executive in 1988. His assessment was dead-on, but he probably failed to appreciate fully the implications. Two decades later GM, once the icon of America's managerial expertise and industrial might, declared bankruptcy.[3]

Governmental organizations may be the most difficult and most resistant to change of all. Not only are they often very large, but they normally also have well-established standards and procedures and are beholden to multiple interests with divergent agendas and priorities. Bureaucratic politics in Washington frequently appear as zero-sum games. Because one organization's gains are perceived, and often are, another's loss, turf wars are more the rule than the exception. The National Security Act of 1947, which established the Department of Defense (DoD) and Central Intelligence Agency (CIA), is an exemplar. Its enactment was so tortuous, and it left in its wake so many scars and so much dissatisfaction, that in the vital arena of national security nothing comparable was attempted for a half century.[4]

Because of the tragedy of September 11, 2001 (9/11), as magnified by the erroneous National Intelligence Estimate (NIE) on Weapons of Mass Destruction (WMD) in Iraq, the momentum for changing how the U.S. Intelligence Community (IC) goes about its business became irresistible. The consensus was that the system was broken and had to be fixed — reformed. Hence Congress entitled the legislation it passed in 2004 the "Intelligence Reform and Terrorism Prevention Act" (IRTPA).[5]

While passed with great fanfare, IRTPA generated little enthusiasm. As is uniformly the case with such legislation, the devil tends to lie in the details. However, in order to expedite passage in the face of so many vested interests and conflicting perspectives, the IRTPA's authors finessed most of the details. They left authorities, responsibilities, divisions of labor, and more (even location) to be decided by future deliberations and decisions. Placed within the context of recent history, this "transition-induced dysfunction," to quote the always quotable Richard Posner, suggested to many observers that the Office of the Director of National Intelligence (ODNI) would evolve into one more bloated bureaucracy which profligately consumed resources and critically undermined essential "speed and precision."[6]

Worse, ODNI was almost certain to generate turf wars not only with the very agencies it was mandated to manage but also with the Pentagon behemoth. The IRTPA did not endow the DNI with the wherewithal to effectively wage these wars. The budget for intelligence activities that supported the military, for example, remained with the DoD. One veteran of America's intelligence establishment constructed a soccer metaphor. He wrote that what the legislation actually did was "send more players onto the field and . . . pump steroids into those already wearing cleats," thereby "adding to the tussles over who is responsible for covering which part of the intelligence terrain" even as it produced "unrealistic expectations."[7] There would be change—but little reform or improvement.

I subscribed to that view. Even as the IRTPA was winding its way through Congress, I was completing a brief history of the CIA. I closely examined the agency's origins in 1947 and subsequent efforts at reform. While not dismissing the possibility that the legislation would improve U.S. intelligence capabilities, I concluded that historical precedent dictated pessimism. I argued at that time and subsequently that the problems that afflicted the U.S. intelligence community were so pervasive, and reflected such an array of dynamics—political, psychological, and cultural—that they were all but impervious to institutional reforms.[8]

Subsequent scholarship, and for that matter much of the informed public's opinion, has been largely consistent with my instinctual prognosis. Enthusiastic assessments of the performance of any of the Directors of National Intelligence (there have already been three), the new institutions established under his authority (most notably the National Counterterrorism and National Counterproliferation Centers), the products for which he is directly responsible (National Intelligence Estimates and the President's Daily Brief), or other components of his office, have been few and far between. Putting aside the vitriolic condemnation of the NIE on Iran's nuclear program by conservative Americans who have historically perceived America's intelligence community as challenged in both its politics and its competence (in the interest of full disclosure, I was a target),[9] even long-time supporters of, and contributors to, America's intelligence were hardly less critical. A former acting CIA deputy director of operations in 2008 wrote that the "DNI has become what intelligence professors feared it would: an unnecessary bureaucratic contraption with an amazingly large staff."[10] The same year another former assistant director of the CIA who served as vice chair of the National Intelligence Council and is the current executive director of the International Association for Intelligence Education, argued that the "dysfunctional structure" produced by IRTPA has "fated" the Intelligence Community to end up a "failed institution."[11] Bipartisan assessments by congressional committees and even the DNI's own Office of the Inspector General have been almost as critical.[12]

In 2007, two leading scholars of intelligence published first-rate books on the subject. They reached the same verdict: IRTPA might produce improvements, but the consequences would be marginal at best. According to Richard Betts, the fault lay not so much in the legislation itself, although it was defective. More fundamentally, the intelligence enterprise—collection, analysis, production, dissemination, and consumption—confronts permanent enemies: incomplete or ambiguous evidence; severe time and resource constraints; cognitive biases and shortcomings; deception and denial; and others. The sum of all the IRTPA reforms may over time contain or push back some of these adverse phenomena, although it is too early to reach a judgment. But "the enemies of intelligence cannot be driven from the field." Consequently, with "disillusionment, backlash, and a drop in public support for intelligence activity" so prevalent, expectations for the reforms should remain low.[13]

Amy Zegart's conclusions are even less sanguine. A decade earlier, Zegart had written that those institutions most responsible for safeguarding America's national security, including the CIA, were "flawed by design."[14] Applying her expertise in organizational theory and intelligence history to the post-9/11 environment, her assessment was sharply critical. She writes that the pathologies that afflicted the IC, particularly the CIA and the Federal Bureau of Investigation (FBI), throughout the Cold War, including inherent organizational defects, bureaucratic self-interest, and fragmentation most prominently, were unaffected by the Cold War's termination. Their persistence explains "why US intelligence agencies failed to adapt to the terrorist threat before September 11, why they have not done much better since then, and why they are unlikely to improve substantially in the future." In her judgment, the "Intelligence Community's worst problems endure." Most of the recent reforms have at best "created halting progress. Some have made matters worse."[15]

There is much to commend in Betts's and Zegart's scholarship. No manner of reform can prevent all intelligence failures, and the more difficult the questions the IC addresses, the lower will be its batting average. Further, the IRTPA reforms were flawed, and to some extent by design. Nevertheless, my exposure to the inner workings of the IC in 2007-08 provided evidence and insight that has escaped notice not only by scholars and journalists, but also by IC veterans. What I experienced, and what I learned from that experience, challenges some of the most basic premises of critics of intelligence reform, their reservations concerning the IRTPA and the establishment of the DNI above all. Change within the IC has been uneven, and what change there has been has not produced universally positive dividends. In a remarkably brief time, nevertheless, intelligence analysis has experienced genuine reform, some of which is radical and even revolutionary. That it has, is one of the IC's best-kept secrets. The intent of this chapter is to reveal the nature of such reform.

The movement, and it is a movement, to reform and thereby improve intelligence analysis goes by the name Analytic Transformation. Analytic Transformation envelopes a myriad of institutional initiatives, beginning with the establishment of a small staff led by the Deputy Director of National Intelligence for Analysis (DDNI/A) which conceived and implemented mechanisms and measures that permeate all 16 elements of the IC.[16] Yet, more fundamentally, Analytic Transformation is a program designed to encourage, as much as mandate, analysts to embrace change, horizontally and vertically throughout the IC workforce. Moreover, and at least indirectly, the same encouragement applies to the collection community itself. The program's name should not evoke associations with Secretary of Defense Donald Rumsfeld's agenda for military transformation while managing the Pentagon. The goal of Analytic Transformation is as simple as it is dramatic: "to get the right analysis to the right people at the right time, in a form they can use." The strategy is equally commonsensical: "to transform the analytic component of our community from a federation of agencies, or a collection of feudal baronies, into a community of analysts."[17]

The principles that underlie this effort are collaboration and integration. Like the goal itself, the words are simple. Still, in the U.S. intelligence community's universe, they signal a revolution. While historians of American intelligence appropriately focus on the key legislative turning points, including but not limited to the National Security Act, the Foreign Intelligence Surveillance Act, the Intelligence Oversight Act, and, of course, the IRTPA, they have all but overlooked the executive orders that were no less and in some respects more pivotal in the community's evolution. Particularly salient is Executive Order (EO) 12333, signed by President Ronald Reagan in December 1981. Amended first in 2004 and again in 2008, EO 12333 allocated power and responsibilities among the agencies, established lines of authority, and otherwise directed how the IC should conduct its activities with respect to the national intelligence effort.[18]

The impetus for the most recent revision of EO 12333 is the confusion and conflict among the agencies' responsibilities and the lines of authority following IRTPA's establishment of the DNI. Because the legislation failed explicitly to provide the DNI with powers required to execute the IRTPA mandates, many of the agencies denied that he had them. The amended version attracted attention because it provides a partial remedy. It vests the DNI with necessary, albeit not yet sufficient, authorities. What has escaped notice is the deletion of one sentence from Part 1 [1.1(a)] of the original EO 12333 that provided the "philosophy" for Analysis: "Maximum emphasis should be given to fostering analytical competition among appropriate elements of the Intelligence Community."[19]

Doubtless in part because it was populated by many veterans and supporters of the CIA's notorious Team B exercise, the Reagan administration ardently promoted competitive analysis. It assumed that the clash of ideas and data produced a kind of dialectical process that enhanced the rigor of estimates and hence increased the likelihood of their accuracy. The IC leadership concurred, blessing competitive analysis as a best practice. In fact, however, its value is ambiguous; the process is vulnerable to manipulation and corruption. What is more, in the IC's competitive culture, knowledge means power. Thus "analytic competition among appropriate elements" is normatively antithetical to information sharing among appropriate elements.[20]

The consequences of cultural as well as institutional and legal barriers to sharing information among agencies became excruciatingly evident in post-mortems on the 9/11 terrorists attacks, which highlighted the poor communication between CIA and the FBI concerning Khalid al Mihdhar and Nawaf al Hazmi. These blunders by themselves were probably enough to induce the IC leadership to supplant competition with integration and collaboration as top priorities. But the motivation behind Analytic Transformation was more basic: the world was very different in 2001-04, than in 1981, let alone 1947.[21] The information and communication revolutions exponentially increased the volume and intricacy of data ("intel"), whether open source or not, that analysts must digest, process, and interpret. Performing those tasks adequately far exceeds the analytical capacity and expertise of any single agency, let alone one office within an agency.

The IC's demographics exacerbate this challenge. The size of the IC's workforce eroded steadily following Watergate and the Church/Pike Committee hearings in the 1970s. The Reagan years were an exception, but the decline accelerated with the peace dividend that America purportedly earned by "winning" the

Cold War. George Tenet committed his tenure as DCI to rebuilding it; he had barely begun when 9/11 arrived. The subsequent hiring frenzy that aimed to compensate for this shortfall produced the "greening" of the IC. In 2007 some 55 percent of the IC's analysts had less than 6 years of experience. Their limited expertise demanded greater interdependence.[22]

Then there is the complexity and disruption that have accompanied the transition from bipolarity to globalization. Attending this transition are new developments, challenges, and threats, many of which are asymmetrical, many of which arise from nonstate actors with transnational reaches, and many of which obscure conventional boundaries between foreign and domestic. Assessing them in order to understand them better, and doing so within the progressively more compressed decisionmaking cycles imposed by policymakers, require innovative analytic approaches that can often benefit from technological advances. Because representatives of "Generation Y" now comprise a large percentage of the analytic workforce, they are more comfortable with, and open to, new techniques that enable collaboration and integration. But for analysts to collaborate, they must be able to locate one another. As late as 2004, when Congress enacted the IRTPA, the IC's front office, such as it was, had virtually no idea how many analysts it managed, let alone on what desks they worked in which home agency. Institutional mechanisms needed to be developed for identifying analysts across the community who possessed the necessary expertise on any given problem. Further, their managers, often the graybeards with much more limited exposure to advanced technology and a cultural aversion to sharing information, had to change their outlooks.

As did the IC's leadership, and in the most fundamental respects. Collectors, most prominently from the CIA's Directorate of Operations (now the National Clandestine Service) and such elements controlled by the Pentagon as the National Security Agency and National Geospatial-Intelligence Agency, had long been kings of the intelligence hill. In the IC, like elsewhere in Washington, influence follows the money, and an analyst costs a pittance compared to an operative in search of human intelligence (HUMINT), not to mention a satellite or ultra-sensitive surveillance system. But in the messy environment of the 21st century, the value of the analyst took a quantum leap. Regardless of the resources committed to collection, and regardless of the instruments and assets available, the volume of data that must be collected in an era of globalization guarantees gaps in that collection. Only analysts' judgments can bridge those gaps. To arrive at sound judgments as expeditiously as possible, moreover, analysts require technologies that can facilitate the search for and the organization of data, identify commonalities and conflicts, and produce parallel benefits that conserve for analysts the time to think.

These dynamics were foremost on Thomas Fingar's mind when in 2005 he began work as the first Deputy Director of National Intelligence for Analysis (dual hatted, he also chaired the National Intelligence Council). A Stanford Ph.D. in Political Science with more than 20 years experience in the IC, Fingar had the right credentials. He also had the right track record. When Carl Ford fell ill in 2002, Fingar, as his principal deputy, assumed the lead of the Department of State's Bureau of Intelligence and Research (INR). In October, 2002, the National Foreign Intelligence Board (subsequently renamed the National Intelligence Board) approved the NIE on Iraq's WMD. INR was the sole IC element to dissent from the basic judgment that Iraq harbored concealed WMD and, perhaps more important, was engaged in a program to reconstitute its nuclear weapons program. Indeed, it was not persuaded that Iraq intended to use the aluminum tubes it sought to acquire for centrifuge rotors. What is significant is that INR did not contradict the NIE assessment. Rather, the INR declared ignorance — that there was insufficient evidence to support the NIE's judgments. What distinguished INR and Fingar was this stout adherence to the most elementary standards of analytic tradecraft — to claim as fact only that which was known to be fact. That criterion became a hallmark of Analytic Transformation.[23]

That Fingar emerged from the Iraq WMD NIE debacle with a distinctive reputation for analytic rigor made him the appropriate choice to head the reform effort. His leadership skills and style made him the inspired choice. Fingar's knowledge of the IC — its processes, its behavior, its culture — was unsurpassed. He appreciated and greatly respected its history and its achievements. But intimately familiar with how the IC worked, somewhat irreverent in his outlook, and innately predisposed to thinking and acting unconventionally, he deemed no procedure or custom sacred and off limits. From his perspective, the normative IC performance was not nearly as poor as critics charged after 9/11 and the Iraq WMD estimate. These snapshots projected a distorted image. Still, there were fundamental areas that demanded remediation. In combination with that demand, public perception, political pressure, and notoriety surrounding the 9/11 and Iraq WMD commissions generated the kind of perfect storm essential to undertaking the reform effort. These opportunities to initiate change in a government institution the size of the IC arise perhaps once in a generation, if that. They last at most a couple of years. Fingar, a workaholic, refused to waste a moment.

Beginning with little more than a vague mandate, Fingar assembled around him a small staff comprised of true believers in the urgent need for reform. Some were senior intelligence officers, others had contributed to the IRTPA, still others were recruited from outside the IC because of their skill sets. Led, encouraged, and energized by Fingar, this staff worked intensely with him to formulate and then promote what soon came to be called Analytic Transformation.

Fingar and his staff, known collectively by the acronym DDNI/A, began at the most elementary level—the analysts themselves. The objective was to identify those analysts across the IC elements that, because of background and expertise, should logically collaborate with one another. What they soon learned, however, was not simply that these analysts were atomized. They were unaccounted for, even within their own agencies. Thus as a cornerstone for Analytic Transformation, DDNI/A constructed an Analytic Resources Catalogue (ARC), a database of information on all IC analysts that indicates each one's expertise, experience, and special skills. From the ARC evolved the Analysts Yellow Pages, a virtual rolodex that enables analysts working on, for example, Iraq or WMD, to find the names, phone numbers, and email addresses of colleagues who have or have had the same or cognate accounts. Such innovations may appear pedestrian. But they addressed an insuperable impediment to collaboration, and in doing so laid a foundation for more dramatic initiatives.[24]

Of these, none were more vital, or counterintuitively more radical, than training—joint training. Analytic training within the IC, as defined by deep immersion in the fundamentals of critical analysis, is itself largely a 21st-century phenomenon. On March 4, 2000, George Tenet dedicated the CIA's Sherman Kent School for Intelligence Analysis. The legendary Kent had proposed its establishment as early as 1953. In the almost half-century interim, instruction provided by the CIA's Office of Training and Education at "the Farm" and elsewhere gave short shrift to critical thinking and structured analytic techniques. The same held true at the few other extant "schoolhouses": the Defense Intelligence Agency's Joint Military Intelligence Training Center (JMITC); the National Defense Intelligence College (chartered in 1962, awards B.S. and M.A. degrees); the Federal Bureau of Investigation Academy; the National Security Agency's National Cryptologic School; and, most recently, the National Geospatial-Intelligence Agency's Academy. However, not only did their quality and curricula vary, but the autonomy of the schoolhouses also reinforced the diffusion of IC analysts. They trained separately, inhabited separate spaces, and produced their separate intelligence products, often from separate sources.[25]

Analysts had to learn to share. They also had to develop the trust in one another that sharing and collaboration require. DDNI/A Fingar understood that unless an analyst from one element has confidence in an analyst from another, she/he will be loath to share information with the other person. Without confidence, moreover, there will be insufficient incentive to collaborate, because the quality of the collaborator's product will be suspect. The answer was joint training in a common, indeed a neutral, environment.

DDNI/A developed, tested, and then managed the poorly named Analysis 101, a foundational course in the critical thinking, structured techniques, and other tradecraft skills that rigorous analysis demands, regardless of the functional or geographic specialization. Following the military aphorism, in Analysis 101 intelligence analysts train the way they fight—collaboratively. Ironically, many of the uniformed leaders in intelligence billets resisted this degree of joint training at the start of the analysts' careers. Adding to this irony, yet reflecting its support for the course's aims, the DIA, which has the resources to sustain the course, took over its management as the DNI's executive agent in October 2008.[26]

Because its purpose is to promote "jointness" as well as to train, Analysis 101 (the JMITC added "Introduction to Critical Thinking and Structured Analysis" to the title) is based on "standards"—in two senses of the word. In the first sense, analysts from the different elements receive standard training, build a standard vocabulary, and identify standard sets of questions. As a consequence, even as they develop a greater appreciation for the distinct contributions of their home agencies, the experiences they share in the classroom with peers from across that IC, especially when working in teams on case studies, tear down the barriers to future collaboration and promote a community ethos. Indeed, they leave the course with a list of names from other elements that they trust and to whom they can reach out for expertise or contacts. Student evaluations and testimonials signal they understand the dynamic and the goal. "The Analysis 101 course supports this new vision and approach," wrote one graduate in reference to the emphasis on collaboration and integration, "by actively promoting future interagency cooperation through a constant and consistent reinforcement of the idea that students from these different agencies will work together not only in the course but will depend on this new coordination model to fully utilize the expertise and resources of the different agencies within the IC to solve problems of mutual concern."[27]

With regard to the second sense of the word, the course also introduces the students to lofty standards of critical thinking. Rather than compelling the analytic workforce, many of whom had only recently graduated from college, to "learn by osmosis," Fingar recalled in an article marking Analysis 101's one thousandth graduate, the course "set[s] the bar high" from the beginning of the analysts' careers. It does this by focusing its syllabus and pedagogy on precise standards of analytic tradecraft. These standards were developed, in consultation with an "Action Group" composed of representatives from all the IC elements, by the ODNI's Office of Analytic Integrity and Standards (AIS) and put into effect through a directive of the DNI applicable to all intelligence agencies. Their products as well as those for which Finger and DDNI/A were directly responsible (NIEs and PDBs) would be subject to the new standards.[28]

The standards — eight in number — reflect and promote the "core principles of analytic tradecraft."[29] Half of these evolved directly from the IRTPA legislation and the reports of the 9/11 and Iraq WMD commissions. They include properly describing the quality and reliability of the products' sources, explicitly expressing uncertainties and qualifying judgments, distinguishing between those judgments and the intelligence that informed them, and articulating different yet plausible assessments or interpretations of the data. Supplementing these standards are others that AIS and its Action Group deemed equally important. These concern the relevance to matters of national security, the logic of the argumentation, the extent to which the product's judgments challenged or revised previous ones, and, of course, accuracy. Merely using these standards as a checklist when writing reports all but assures improvement in their quality, consequently engendering the confidence of other analysts and as well as consumers in that quality. Moreover, the standards serve as cues for the analysts to think more attentively and sensitively about their own thinking, thereby intensifying its rigor. The students' exposure to such structured methods as Analysis of Competing Hypotheses and Argument Mapping, accompanied by technological tools, intensified that rigor further.[30]

The intention of Intelligence Community Directive (ICD) 203 is to sharpen the critical thinking that underlies intelligence products; a supplementary ICD aimed to increase the transparency of those products. ICD 206 requires that analysts provide "consistent and structured sourcing information" for all disseminated analytic products. [31] In other words, any intelligence product intended for distribution beyond the office that generated it must, like work of the scholarly community, include citations of sources, original not secondary, on which the products' claims are based. ICD 206 mandates that these citations, which must take the form of endnotes to avoid interrupting the flow of the text and also to facilitate their removal for purposes of sanitization, conform to a precise style to make certain that they convey to the reader, whether another analyst or consumer, the sourcing information needed not only for retrieval but also for evaluation. Indeed, the ICD encourages analysts to acquire from collectors insight into the nature and reliability of the source and add this to the note as a source descriptor (or when feasible incorporate it into the text). Doing so reduces the potential for exaggerating the credibility of a judgment based on misleading or deceptive input. Further, a source summary statement that concisely encapsulates "the key sources of information used in the product, addressing such strengths and limitations of available information, notable inconsistencies in reporting, important information gaps, or other factors that the producing organization deems relevant," must appear conspicuously. Given current training, the likelihood of a product relying on outdated intelligence is remote. That the analyst must now advertise this reliance makes this scenario even less likely. Of course, extraordinary and mission-critical circumstances might make adherence impractical and even impossible. For such cases, the ICD establishes a procedure for the IC element to request a waiver, or even an exemption for an entire product line. Moreover, if for purposes of dissemination a product must be sanitized or downgraded, a fully-sourced version must be retained for future reference.

ICD 203 and 206, which taken together address the fundamentals of tradecraft and transparency, are at the very heart of Analytic Transformation. Indeed, the success of the reform effort will be judged according to the effectiveness of the implementation of the two directives. The challenges are immense. Those who draft intelligence products, and their managers up the line, are not all graduates of Analysis 101. They are more senior—many are are of long tenure. Their training, which in large part came informally through mentors, was very different. To many analysts of the old school, sourcing, let alone this degree of detailed sourcing, takes too much time. Worse, according to their *welt-anschauung*, sourcing is anathema to the imperative that overrides everything else: protecting sources and methods. In fact, to adhere to the IC standards virtually without exception, IC veterans need to unlearn ingrained behavior. Seasoned analysts, Deputy Director Fingar came to recognize, had "a difficult time stating their assumptions up front, explicitly explaining their logic, and, in the end, indentifying unambiguously for policymakers what they do not know." While openly conceding a gap in information is necessary, it is not sufficient. Analysts must learn how to "weigh what you know against what you don't know," adds one of Fingar's deputies, and how to "express uncertainty and develop confidence levels in the information and findings."[32]

As a consequence, the purpose of the IC Analytic Standards goes beyond serving as the building blocks for Analysis 101. ICD 203 mandated that the Standards constitute the "basis for evaluation of the analytic production of the IC, and be included in analysis teaching modules and case studies throughout the IC." This directive is based on the paragraph in section 1019 of the IRTPA requiring the DNI to assign an individual or entity the responsibility of regularly performing "detailed reviews of finished intelligence products or other analytic products by [any] element or elements of the intelligence community." The directive provides the authority for AIS's evaluation of more than a thousand products each over the past 3 years. In doing so, AIS identified best practices and developed a hierarchical scale for each Standard. For example, it is *good* to provide alternative analyses and to clearly articulate estimates of probabilities, but it is *outstanding* to indicate the signposts that will signal the likely evolution of each alternative, especially ones with low probability but potentially high impact. Products that explicitly assess the depth and reliability of the reporting on which the product depended, gaps in that reporting, and the assumptions the analysts used to bridge those gaps (not to be confused with the "expanded methodology" and the subsequent "knowns, known unknowns, and unknown unknowns" catch phrase attributed to Donald Rumsfeld), receive high marks based on multiple standards.[33]

The evaluators then brief the results of these evaluations to the heads of each of the agencies' training units as well as their directors of analysis. They also present workshops to different offices. At least as significant, throughout 2008 they consulted with each IC element in establishing its in-house evaluation program in order to create a multiplier effect. This signal achievement was completed by the fall of 2008. The evaluations have become instruments to train increasing numbers of senior analysts throughout the IC. This training will benefit further from the approaching completion of a compendium of best practices and lessons learned from the evaluations, to be titled *Insights into Applying the Intelligence Community's Analytic Standards: A Guide to Best Practices*.[34]

Has this effort transformed intelligence analysis? It is too early to tell, but the signs are encouraging. Although analysts still stumble, particularly over some of the standards, and the training needed to satisfy the sourcing requirements has just begun, the evaluation grades for all types of products are trending in the right direction. What is more, the results of the few assessments of performance related to the eighth Tradecraft Standard appear positive.[35] Accuracy is, of course, the gold standard for analysts. Yet, evaluating accuracy is very hard. The degree of difficulty is a variable, as is the required time. If, for example, an intelligence-based warning precipitates successful preventive or preemptive measures, an accurate prediction will, of course, be retrospectively inaccurate. Nevertheless, based on the small set of studies undertaken, there does seem to be a correlation between outstanding tradecraft and the accuracy of the product. Many future estimates will surely prove to be wrong. Still, for intelligence producers and consumers, the preliminary results of the evaluations are very good news. Perhaps even better news, in the long run, is the increased attention paid to tradecraft throughout the IC, and the sense of collegiality, even fraternity, that this attention has generated. Analysts from across the IC proudly wear laminated cards emblazoned with the IC Analytic Standards on their lanyards—signaling their membership in the same "club." This degree of team-mindedness is unprecedented in the history of U.S. intelligence.

Identifying collaboration and integration as the benchmarks of Analytic Transformation compelled DDNI/A Fingar and his staff to tackle impediments as fundamental as training and tradecraft but over which they exercised less control. In particular, they had to confront pervasive information hoarding. "Inadequate information sharing is a major impediment to effective IC performance," reads the 2008 report on the Director of National Intelligence's "Critical Intelligence Community Management Challenges" by the ODNI's Office of the Inspector General. The report cites IRTPA's requirement that the DNI enact reforms "to ensure maximum availability of and access to intelligence information and to establish policies and procedures to resolve conflicts between the need to share intelligence information and the need to protect intelligence sources and methods." It concludes that the DNI has failed to satisfy this requirement. Consequently, analysts still must rely on "personal relationships with counterparts to acquire much of their intelligence data." More pernicious, "Agencies responsible for developing collection systems," primarily but not exclusively the CIA (HUMINT), NSA (signals intelligence - SIGINT), and NGA (imagery intelligence - IMINT), continue to control and limit access to data and products essential to analysis across the IC." The lack of interoperability among many of the IC elements' respective IT systems exacerbates these problems.[36]

The IG's report is well-founded. Since the coin of the realm for intelligence is information, possession of it remains pivotal to the IC's internal balance of power. Accordingly, the communal ethos has still not gained full traction, and individual agencies thus remain more predisposed to hoard than to share. Consequently, in December 2007, the DNI approved an Intelligence Community Policy Memorandum emphasizing that each IC element, and each office and individual within each element, has a "responsibility to provide" intelligence information to all customers (including analysts) who require that information. Theoretically, this memorandum renders obsolete the "Need to Know" culture that poses such an obstacle to sharing. But in practice, the result is far from optimal. The memorandum states that the responsibility to provide information "requires that the IC create the appropriate tension to more effectively balance the 'need to share intelligence' with the requisite 'need to protect' sources and methods." Not surprisingly, however, given the degree of difficulty, it neither defines "appropriate tension" nor provides guidance on how to achieve that more "effective balance." Predictably, then, since analysts and collectors are much better trained in the need to protect sources and methods than in the secure procedures to share, and that they are denied rewards for sharing that even remotely counter-balance the penalties for divulging, and that they do not receive direction from the DNI or front office that if conflicts exist that they should err on the side of "need to share," those analysts and collectors are understandably conservative in fulfilling their responsibility to share. Intelligence agencies have long institutional memories, especially regarding when a source or method was once compromised. Only a few have even begun to record success stories produced from information sharing.[37]

So intractable are these problems that the title to IC Directive 501 was changed from "Information Sharing" to "Discovery and Dissemination or Retrieval of Information within the Intelligence Community." The revised title reflects the ICD's more limited scope. It does underscore the principle of "responsibility to provide," emphasizing that IC elements are "stewards," not owners, of information. It also calls both raw intelligence and analytic products "national assets." Nevertheless, the requirement ensures only that information is "discoverable" by "authorized personnel." Retrieving and accessing the information that is discovered still entails surmounting the many obstacles that inhere in a seemingly immutable classification system. In addition, the discoverability of the intelligence, raw and finished, depends on automated means that have not yet been fully developed.[38]

DDNI/A Fingar recognized that information sharing is integral to Analytic Transformation. But without the cooperation of other directorates within the ODNI and the individual elements that comprise the IC, DDNI/A's reach is limited. Nevertheless, Fingar, relying heavily on Michael Wertheimer, his assistant for Analytic Transformation and Technology, placed the promotion of information sharing through both attitudinal change and technological innovation at the very top of his agenda. The ODNI's Inspector General singled out Wertheimer's efforts as among the very few "significant achievements in information sharing." But to many of the IC elements, Wertheimer is "the most dangerous man in U.S. intelligence."[39]

That is because Wertheimer, notwithstanding his more than 2 decades of immersion in the IC culture as a cryptologist of the NSA, is a risk-taker — one who, particularly after 9/11, lost all patience with the various fiefdoms' excessive classification of and monopolies over intelligence. With the DDNI/A's unqualified support, he proclaimed simply that notwithstanding the IC's traditions and standard operating procedures, "We are going to share more." There is no other option: "We can't afford the kinds of mistakes that we're making based on the way we're doing business today," he said. Wertheimer prefers the term "Analytic Liberation" to "Analytic Transformation" because it signals "unleashing" the analytic community's potential.[40]

Wertheimer was DDNI/A's point man in the drafting of ICD 501. He would have preferred a more robust directive, and without his contributions, it doubtless would have been more limited. Further, Wertheimer's focus has been less on policy, which he could influence only moderately, but rather on the architecture of information sharing, over which he could exercise more authority. This made it feasible for the analysts themselves, where the dissemination of information and ideas was concerned, to exercise more authority. IRTPA requires the creation of a single Information Sharing Environment (ISE), which is designed to facilitate the dissemination of information particularly related to terrorism. For this purpose, there was to be a program manager (Chief Information Officer), a council, and attendant offices. Implementation has proven predictably difficult, and the CIO's office has foundered. But Wertheimer's office within DDNI/A launched several interrelated initiatives with the potential to produce extremely far-reaching consequences.[41]

Chief among these is the creation of a Library of National Intelligence (LNI). In collaboration with the CIA, DDNI/A constructed in cyberspace the first authoritative repository for disseminated intelligence throughout the IC, regardless of its classification and origin. On deposit in the LNI will be the fully sourced versions of all finished intelligence, complemented by a finder's guide consisting of a virtual card catalogue that is classified at the lowest possible level and contains summary abstracts of products. As now authorized by ICD 501, analysts can discover and *request* access to these products. Whether they can successfully access them will depend on individual levels of clearance and the products' security guidelines. But even if denied access, analysts will benefit from knowing the existence and dates of analyses on a subject. No less important, they will learn whether there has been no analysis. Further, an analyst without the appropriate clearance can request special access to the product or ask for a sanitized version.

The LNI was launched in November 2007; by the end of its first year about half of the elements in the IC had taken the measures their internal requirements demanded in order to submit products to it. Although still undergoing testing, by the beginning of 2009, the LNI had in principle achieved the capacity to make available some 800,000 products for analysts to share across the IC, and it was adding some 20,000 products each week. It was also making progress toward meeting another vital need. Through Catalyst, a data program still under development, key data such as names of persons, places, and organizations will be tagged (metadata tagging) in such a way that they are searchable. This will allow analysts to extract such data from the diverse welter of intelligence sources without having to collate and read the individual products and their documentary sources. (Metadata tagging will also enable the linking of finished intelligence with stored raw reporting.) The Catalyst program, therefore, can help the analyst cope with both the volume of information and its security restrictions. Further, metadata tagging will not only produce additional community-wide standards with regard to identifying attributes, but in conjunction with tracking card catalogue requests, it will allow collectors to determine which sources are appearing most frequently in finished intelligence. This correlation will assist in the formulation of research strategies.[42]

Whereas joint training in IC-wide standards is the "front end" of the reform cycle for the production of intelligence, the LNI is the "back end." In between is the analytic process itself—that phase during which analysts are producing. This is the phase when collaboration is most vital—and yet most difficult. Analysts are sequestered in their respective agencies. To facilitate collaboration among analysts from different agencies, DDNI/A, inspired by the success of MySpace, Facebook, and their web rivals, developed a classified "social" networking website. Tested in early 2008, and then redesigned dramatically in response to feedback, A-Space went on line in September 2008.

A-Space built on two previous DDNI/A initiatives. Intellipedia, the IC's variant of Wikipedia, began as a pilot in 2005, was up and running the next year, and is now heavily used. With different editions available in Top Secret, Secret, and Unclassified environments, it allows tens of thousands of users to collaborate in producing, expanding, and editing articles. What is more, because qualified consumers can also access and indeed contribute to Intellipedia, it fosters interaction between the IC and its customers. A parallel initiative was the establishment of communities of interest (COIs). These are secure web-based environments in which analysts, collectors, and managers from different agencies with common accounts come together in a virtual environment to share their ideas — and to some extent their data.

A-Space did not replace either Intellipedia or COIs. But to a degree, it synthesized them and thereby took each to a higher level of utility. Unlike Intellipedia, A-Space is available only to intelligence analysts, and even then only to those with a Top Secret/Sensitive Compartmented Information (TS/SCI) security clearance (a version at least at the Secret level is planned). Like both Intellipedia and COIs, the secure workspace allows analysts to share ideas and collaborate. But unlike the others, A-Space serves as a well-guarded gateway to highly classified sources and databases. Indeed, access to A-Space is so tightly controlled that agencies have received waivers to post data that otherwise are subject to regulations preven-ting their being shared.[43] Analysts can consequently not only brainstorm as they develop their thinking, but also actually access and share the intelligence as well as the expertise that drives that thinking.

Thus A-Space offers analysts an opportunity, and potentially an incentive, to think out loud by posting their insights and even sourced rough drafts for comments by their peers. Colleagues from other agencies can critique these works in progress, challenging key assumptions, offering alternative analyses, even drawing attention to supplementary or conflicting data. Because of the process of managerial review, the coordination required before publication, and the difficulty of finalizing prior to a virtual peer review, it is unlikely that A-Space will evolve into a site for producing finished intelligence (although this has been attempted). But it can play a valuable role in the drafting phases, as well as offering a forum for exchanging views on all matters of tradecraft methodology and attendant issues.[44]

It will be beneficial if A-Space is opened to IC's collection community. Collectors should be familiar with analysts' thinking, and vice versa. But even without A-Space and other shared environments, the nexus between analysis and collection is tightening. In forging this relationship, the office of Analytic Mission Management (AMM) has played a catalytic role. DDNI/A Fingar recognized that the addition of an exploding number of nonstate-centered asymmetrical threats to the data overload that accompanied the information and communication revolutions demanded IC-wide conversations among analysts. This addition likewise required, as Fingar clearly saw, that collectors participate in those conversations. Collectors and collection systems could no longer resemble, to use Fingar's metaphor, "vacuum cleaners on steroids," drowning analysts in such oceans of data that they cannot possibly process it. Moreover, the data collected was not necessarily correlated to the most pressing questions of the analysts — or the policymakers, warfighters, and first responders. To improve the quality of analysis, collection had to focus on filling the most vital information gaps.[45]

DDNI/A Fingar charged AMM with tracking the allocation of analytic resources across the community so as to better align them with high-priority targets. Not all IC elements should work the same targets. AMM seeks to orchestrate a division of labor driven by expertise and capabilities. To order those targets hierarchically, moreover, the office also engages in collaborative dialogues for the purpose of developing the National Intelligence Priorities Framework (NIPF). Updated semiannually, the NIPF establishes "objectives, priorities, and guidance to the IC to ensure timely and effective collection, processing, analysis, and dissemination of national intelligence." AMM operates both at and below the level of this superstructure. On behalf of the DDNI/A, it oversees the formulation and revisions of the NIPF. Concurrently, it also keeps close tabs on the production process in order to assess the quality and coverage of finished intelligence on the highest priority targets, to identify as precisely as possible disabling gaps that are impairing analyses, and to coordinate with the collection community for the purpose of closing those gaps.[46]

AMM's vital role in coordinating the analytic and collection communities has become increasingly institutionalized. In late 2007, the DNI set up the National Intelligence Coordination Center (NIC-C). The deputy directors of both analysis and collection were represented on it in order to facilitate their collaboration. Finally, Analysis and Collection were formally joined. Previously they had been linked to some extent through the Mission Management system, manifested most notably in IRTPA's establishment of the National Counterterrorism and National Counterproliferation Centers, but also evident in the specific country mission managers designated by the DNI on Iran, North Korea, and Cuba/Venezuela. AMM essentially provided mission management for all other topics—acting as a liaison between the analysts and collectors. However, ICD 207, the directive on the National Intelligence Council, assigned these responsibilities to the NIC's National Intelligence Officers. Because the NIO offices have paltry staffs, AMM provides critical support. In this capacity, as well as through its responsibilities to the NIPF and NIC-C, AMM is fundamental to implementing another pillar of Analytic Transformation: *Analysis must drive collection, not the other way around.*[47]

The establishment of the ODNI is, of course, not a panacea, and DDNI/A, which comprises but a small percentage of the IC's workforce, resources, and budget, is but the tail wagging the dog. Predictably, then, severe challenges remain.[48] The culture of distinctiveness (often almost mythic in its grip) and competition among the elements remain pervasive, often defiantly so. The preponderant influence on and within the IC of the military, with its tradition of separateness and branding that continues to resist the spirit of the Goldwater-Nichols reorganization, reinforces this culture.[49] The consequences are extremely detrimental for information sharing, especially when juxtaposed with a reflexive disposition toward secretiveness, and the widespread belief that secrets are the key ingredients of bureaucratic power. Dynamic, even aggressive, leadership from the DNI is absolutely essential to overcome the many sources of resistance. But for reasons that include an uncertainty about authorities, a fear of projecting the image of one more cannibalizing institution, and a recognition that all but one of the IC elements report to a cabinet-level official, DNI leadership has been tentative. Michael McConnell's successor as DNI, Admiral Dennis C. Blair, "came to the job determined to cement the intelligence chief's authority over 16 disparate spy agencies." The consequence has been cold war with the CIA, the outcome of which remains undecided. The DNI's directives will prove effective only when the elements accept them in spirit and in principle as well as practice.[50]

In addition to all these institutional obstacles to reform is their degree of difficulty. Finding the proper balance between sharing information and protecting sources and methods is hard. Penetrating hard targets to collect reliable intelligence is notoriously hard. Reaching confident judgments by evaluating what is known against what is not known is hard. Finding accurate answers to the tough as opposed to easy questions is hard. Providing smart and experienced customers with information and insight beyond what they already have is hard. Tailoring intelligence to specific customer sets with specific needs and security clearances is hard. Intelligence analysis is an art, not a science; there is a difference between a puzzle and a mystery. The best intelligence can do is narrow the boundaries of uncertainty. It cannot eliminate it, and thus there will be intelligence failures. Even when an estimate gets it right, the judgment is rarely so clear-cut as to satisfy a conflicted consumer or persuade him or her to reverse course or take decisive action.[51]

Still, the initiatives that have largely gone unnoticed in the public sphere suggest that the intelligence-reform glass is half full. The objective of IRTPA is to improve the quality of America's national intelligence, and its quality has improved. While it would be an exaggeration to claim that all intelligence reports are now based on all sources of information, that is a standard to which the IC explicitly aspires. Further, products are based on more sources of information, the quality and reliability of which are exponentially more transparent. Analysts make unequivocal both what they know and what inferences that they drew from what they know in order to provide judgments about what they do not know. Without giving an impression of false precision, they indicate the confidence levels that they have in their inferences and judgments as well as articulating alternative scenarios. When there is dissent or disagreement, the customer is informed of it.

Even if not perfect, moreover, there is greater collaboration and integration throughout the IC. In addition, analysts are now not only authorized but also encouraged to reach out to expertise wherever it can be located—in universities, in think tanks, in industry, in the scientific community, and elsewhere, particularly if those experts are likely to challenge orthodoxy.[52] The IC still suffers from limited language capabilities and insufficient training facilities, but it no longer conceals such inadequacies and is committed to addressing them. Most fundamental of all, the IC, as a community, recognizes that it must improve, and the contemporary environment lends great urgency to that imperative. In light of the caliber and commitment of the personnel, that recognition gives cause for optimism.

ENDNOTES - CHAPTER 4

1. Remarks by Dr. Thomas Fingar at the DNI's Information Sharing Conference and Technology Exposition, August 21-25, 2006, available from *www.dni.gov/speeches/20060821_2_speech.pdf*.

2. I thank Jeremy Schmidt for his very helpful research, and James Marchio, Randall McCall, and Karl Pieragostini for their insightful comments and criticism. From September 4, 2007, through December 31, 2008, I served as Assistant Deputy Director of National Intelligence for Analytic Integrity and Standards, and Analytic Ombudsman for the Office of the Director of National Intelligence. Nevertheless, the views expressed in this publication are my own and do not imply endorsement by the Office of the Director of National Intelligence or any other U.S. Government agency.

3. Elmer Johnson quoted in David Brooks, "The Quagmire Ahead," *New York Times*, June 1, 2009. On General Motors as a model of good management, see David Farber, *Sloan Rules: Alfred P. Sloan and the Triumph of General Motors*, Chicago, IL: University of Chicago Press, 2002.

4. Thomas F. Troy, *Donovan and the CIA*, Frederick, MD: University Publications of America, 1981; David Rudgers, *Creating the Secret State: The Origins of the Central Intelligence Agency, 1943-1947*, Lawrence: University of Kansas Press, 2000.

5. Public Law 108-458, *The Intelligence Reform and Terrorism Prevention Act*, December 17, 2004; available from *travel.state.gov/pdf/irtpa2004.pdf*.

6. Fred Kaplan, "You Call That a Reform Bill?" *Slate*, December 7, 2004, available from *www.slate.com/id/2110767*; Joshua Sinai, "Countering Terrorism: Reform of Intelligence Not the Answer," *Washington Times*, April 19, 2005; Richard Posner, "Important Job, Impossible Position," *New York Times*, February 9, 2005.

7. Philip Shenon, "Next Round is Set to Push to Reorganize Intelligence: Turf Wars and Debates are Expected," *New York Times*, December 20, 2004; Philip Shenon, "The Beast That Feeds

on Boxes: Bureaucracy," *New York Times*, April 10, 2005; John Brennan, "Is This Intelligence? We Added Players But Lost Control of the Ball," *Washington Post*, November 20, 2005.

8. Richard H. Immerman, "A Brief History of the CIA," *The Central Intelligence Agency: Security Under Scrutiny*, Athan Theoharis, *et al.*, eds., Westport, CT: Greenwood Publishing Group, 2006, pp. 79-85; Richard H. Immerman, "Intelligence and Strategy: Historicizing Psychology, Politics, and Policy," *Diplomatic History*, Vol. 32, January 2008, pp. 1-23.

9. See, for example, John R. Bolton, "The Flaws in the Iran Report," *Washington Post*, December 6, 2007; Henry Kissinger, "Misreading the Iran Report: Why Spying and Policymaking Don't Mix," *Washington Post*, December 13, 2007. For criticisms that target this author, see Gabriel Schoenfeld, "If Michael Moore Had a Security Clearance: How Did the Rabid Ideologue Richard Immerman Get Put in Charge of the 'Standards and Integrity' of the Intelligence Community?" *Weekly Standard*, March 3, 2008; Gabriel Schoenfeld, "The Real Bush Intelligence Failure," *Wall Street Journal*, April 3, 2008; Bill Gertz, "Inside the Ring," *Washington Times*, March 14, 2008; The Key Judgments of the NIE, "Iran: Nuclear Intentions and Capabilities," November 2007, is available from *www.dni.gov/press_releases/20071203_release.pdf*.

10. Jack Devine, "An Intelligence Reform Reality Check," *Washington Post*, February 18, 2008.

11. Mark M. Lowenthal, "The Real Intelligence Failure: Spineless Spies," *Washington Post*, May 25, 2008. See also Melvin A. Goodman, "The Colossal Failure of the Office of the Director of National Intelligence," *The Public Record*, April 2, 2009, available from *www.pubrecord.org/commentary/811-the-colossal-failure-of-the-office-of-the-director-of-national-intelligence.html*.

12. Scott Shane, "In New Job, Spymaster Draws Bipartisan Criticism," *New York Times*, April 20, 2006; Mark Mazzetti, "Report Faults Pace of Intelligence Overhaul," *New York Times*, July 28, 2006; Office of the Director of National Intelligence, Office of the Inspector General, *Critical Intelligence Community Management Challenges*, November 12, 2008, available from *www.globalsecurity.org/intell/library/reports/2008/081112-oig-intel-report.pdf*.

13. Richard K. Betts, *Enemies of Intelligence: Knowledge & Power in American National Security*, New York: Columbia, 2007, pp. 19-52, 183-84.

14. Amy B. Zegart, *Flawed by Design: The Evolution of the CIA, JCS, and NSC*, Stanford, CA: Stanford University Press, 1999.

15. Amy B. Zegart, *Spying Blind: The CIA, the FBI, and the Origins of 9/11*, Princeton, NJ: Princeton University Press, 2007, pp. 59, 182.

16. Equally affected by the initiatives, of course, are the National Counterterrorism and Counterproliferation Centers (NCTC and NCPC) and offices directly responsible to the DDNI/A such as the National Intelligence Council (NIC) and President's Daily Brief (PDB). Increasingly, moreover, Analytic Transformation is extending to the state, local, and tribal law enforcement communities.

17. Thomas Fingar, Preface to *Analytic Transformation: Unleashing the Potential of a Community of Analysts*, September 1, 2008, available from *odni.gov/content/AT_Digital%2020080923.pdf*; Fingar, "Remarks at the DNI's Information Sharing Conference."

18. Executive Order (EO) 12333, "United States Intelligence Activities," December 4, 1981, available from *www.archives.gov/federal-register/codification/executive-order/12333.html*, Part I. See also Executive Order 12333, United States Intelligence Activities (As amended by Executive Orders 13284 [2003], 13355 [2004] and 13470 [2008]), July 30, 2008, available from *www.fas.org/irp/offdocs/eo/eo-12333-2008.pdf*.

19. EO 12333, Part I, 1.1(a).

20. "Soviet Strategic Objectives, An Alternative View (Report of Team 'B')," December 1, 1976, available from *www.faqs.org/cia/docs/46/0000278531/SOVIET-STRATEGIC-OBJECTIVES-AN-ALTERNATE-VIEW-(REPORT-OF-TEAM-%22B.html*; Anne Kahn, *Killing Détente: The Right Attacks the CIA*, College Park: Pennsylvania State University Press, 1998; Gordon R. Mitchell, "Team B Intelligence Coups," *Quarterly Journal of Speech*, Vol. 92, May 2006, pp. 144-173.

21. Albeit without much success, fostering integration and collaboration had, in fact, been a chief priority of George Tenet prior to 9/11. See Douglas F. Garthoff, *Directors of Central Intelligence as Leaders of the U.S. Intelligence Community, 1946-2005*, Washington, DC: Potomac Books, 2007, pp. 256-64.

22. *The 9/11 Commission Report: Final Report of the National Commission on Terrorist Attacks Upon the United States*, New York: Norton, 2004, pp. 266-76; *Report of the Joint Inquiry into the Terrorist Attacks of September 11, 2001*, Washington, DC: The House Permanent Select Committee on Intelligence and the Senate Select Committee on Intelligence, December 2002, pp. 315-24; 355-68, available from *www.gpoaccess.gov/serialset/creports/pdf/fullreport_errata.pdf*; James Risen, "Failures on Terrorism Are Seen Shaping Tenet's Legacy," *New York Times*, June 4, 2004; Transcript of Remarks and Q&A by Thomas Fingar, Commonwealth Club, San Francisco, CA, February 14, 2008 (author's possession).

23. National Intelligence Estimate, Iraq's Continuing Programs for Weapons of Mass Destruction, October 30, 2002, available from *www.fas.org/irp/cia/product/iraq-wmd-nie.pdf*.

24. Fingar, *Analytic Transformation*, p. 16.

25. Remarks of the Director of Central Intelligence, George J. Tenet, at the Dedication of the Sherman Kent School, May 4, 2000, available from *www.cia.gov/news-information/speeches-testimony/2000/dci_speech_05052000.html*.

26. Director of National Intelligence Michael McConnell memorandum to the IC, September 22, 2008 (author's possession).

27. Memorandum from [name omitted] intelligence research specialist to the deputy director of his analytical center, January 16, 2009, (author's permission, used by permission of the Office of the Director of National Intelligence and the appropriate agency).

28. Michael Birmingham, "Analyze This," *The Spotlight*, Vol. 28, December 10, 2008; Intelligence Community Directive (ICD) 203, *Analytic Standards*, effective June 21, 2007, available from *www.fas.org/irp/dni/icd/icd-203.pdf*.

29. There were, in fact five Analytic Standards: (1) objectivity, (2) independent of political considerations, (3) timeliness, (4) based on all available sources of intelligence, and (5) exhibits proper standards of analytic tradecraft. ICD 203 broke this last standard into four, producing eight tradecraft standards. They formed the basis of Analysis 101.

30. ICD 203, 2; Richard J. Heuer, Jr., *Psychology of Intelligence*, Washington, DC: Center for the Study of Intelligence, 1999, pp. 95-110; Richard J. Heuer, Jr., "Computer-Aided Analysis of Competing Hypotheses," in, Roger Z. George and James B. Bruce, eds., *Analyzing Intelligence: Origins, Obstacles, and Innovations*, Washington, DC: Georgetown University Press, 2008, pp. 251-65; Tim van Gelder, "What Is Argument Mapping," Blog, February 17, 2009, available from *timvangelder.com/2009/02/17/what-is-argument-mapping/*.

31. Intelligence Community Directive 206, *Sourcing Requirements for Disseminated Analytic Products*, effective October 17, 2007, available from *www.dni.gov/electronic_reading_room/ICD%20 206,%20Sourcing%20Requirements.pdf*; Bob Drogin, *Curveball: Spies, Lies, and the Man Behind Them: How American Went to War in Iraq*, New York: Random House, 2007. The data in the balance of this paragaph is also taken from Directive 206.

32. The quotes in this paragraph are extracted from Michael Birmingham's "Analyze This."

33. See ICD 203; and IRTPA, Sec. 1019 (b) (1) (A). On Rumsfeld's expanded methodology and catch phrase, see John Diamond, *The CIA and the Culture of Failure: U.S. Intelligence from the End of the Cold War to the Invasion of Iraq*, Stanford, CA: Stanford University Press, 2008, pp. 271-73.

34. U.S. Intelligence Community, *500-Day Plan, Integration and Collaboration: Follow-up Report*, January 16, 2009, available from *www.dni.gov/500-day-plan/500%20Day%20Plan%20Follow%20 Up%20Report%20part%201.pdf*; James Marchio, email correspondence with author, June 1, 2009 (author's possession).

35. See endnote 29.

36. The quotations are from the Office of the Inspector General, *Critical Intelligence Community Management Challenges*, pp. 3-4.

37. Intelligence Community Policy Memorandum 2007-200-2, *Preparing Intelligence to Meet the Intelligence Community's "Responsibility to Provide,"* effective December 11, 2007, available from *www.fas.org/irp/dni/icpm/2007-200-2.pdf.*

38. Intelligence Community Directive 501, *Discovery and Dissemination or Retrieval of Information within the Intelligence Community*, effective January 21, 2009, available from *www.dni.gov/electronic_reading_room/ICD_501.pdf.*

39. Office of the Inspector General, *Critical Intelligence Community Management Challenges*, p. 5; Shane Harris, "Intelligence Veteran Aims to Motivate Young Analysts," *National Journal*, September 24, 2007, available from *www.govexec.com/dailyfed/0907/092407nj1.htm.*

40. Harris, "Intelligence Veteran." Wertheimer's office oversaw the production of the brochure *Analytic Transformation*, the subtitle of which is "Unleashing the Potential of a Community of Analysts." See n. 17 of the present chapter.

41. IRTPA, section 1016.

42. *Analytic Transformation*, pp. 7, 9. There is little information on the Library of National Intelligence accessible to the public.

43. For example, Originator Controlled (ORCON) remains in effect throughout the IC and has in some cases been integral to binding agreements reached between individual agencies and foreign governments. Therefore, while agencies will not consent to disseminate data which originated with them and they accordingly control, they have designated A-Space to be an exception and waived this restriction with regard to sharing data on it.

44. Scott Shane, "Logged in and Sharing Gossip, er, Intelligence," *New York Times*, September 2, 2007.

45. For the comments and views expressed by Fingar in this paragraph, see his "Remarks at the DNI's Information Sharing Conference."

46. Intelligence Community Directive 204, *Roles and Responsibilities of the National Intelligence Priorities Framework*, effective September 13, 2007, available from *www.fas.org/irp/dni/icd/icd-204.pdf*.

47. Intelligence Community Directive 207, *National Intelligence Council*, effective June 9, 2008, available from *www.dni.gov/electronic_reading_room/ICD_207.pdf*.

48. Nancy Bernkopf Tucker, "The Cultural Revolution in Intelligence: Interim Report," *Washington Quarterly*, Spring 2008, pp. 47-61.

49. Public Law 99-433, Goldwater-Nichols Department of Defense Reorganization Act of 1986, October 1, 1986, available from *https://digitalndulibrary.ndu.edu/cdm4/document.php?CISOROOT=/nduldpub&CISOPTR=674&CISOSHOW=587*.

50. Mark Mazzetti, "Turf Battles on Intelligence Pose Test for Spy Chiefs," *New York Times*, June 9, 2009; Pamela Hess, "CIA, Intel Director Locked in Spy Turf Battle," Federal News Radio, May 27, 2009, available from *www.federalnewsradio.com/?nid=27&sid=1684040*.

51. Gregory F. Treverton, "Risks and Riddles," *Smithsonian Magazine*, June 2007, available from *www.smithsonianmag.com/people-places/presence_puzzle.html*; Robert Jervis, "The Politics and Psychology of Intelligence and Intelligence Reform," in James P. Pfiffner and Mark Phythian, eds., *Intelligence and National Security Policymaking on Iraq: British and American Perspectives*, College Station: Texas A&M University Press, 2008, p. 167. See also Roger Z. George and James B. Bruce, eds., *Analyzing Intelligence: Origins, Obstacles, and Innovations*, Washington, DC: Georgetown University Press, 2008.

52. Intelligence Community Directive 205, *Analytic Outreach*, effective July 16, 2008, available from *www.dni.gov/electronic_reading_room/ICD%20205.pdf*.

CHAPTER 5

REFORMING THE NATIONAL SECURITY PROCESS IN A GLOBALIZING WORLD

James Goldgeier

For 4 decades, the U.S. national security apparatus was geared toward the threat posed by the Soviet Union. Military planners worried about combating a Red Army onslaught, diplomats negotiated the technical details of arms control agreements, and the intelligence community tried to discern Moscow's intentions and capabilities.

Then it was all over. Soviet leader Mikhail Gorbachev announced a significant unilateral reduction in military capabilities at the United Nations (UN) in December 1988; this was followed by the withdrawal of Soviet troops from Afghanistan in February 1989 and then the stunning fall of the Berlin Wall later that year. Two years after communism collapsed in Eastern Europe, the Soviet Union itself imploded, leaving 15 newly independent countries in its wake.

The end of the Cold War and the collapse of the Soviet Union coincided with the onset of globalization. In fact, it was the inability of the Soviet command economy to adapt to the information technology revolution that had played such a big role in Gorbachev's desperate efforts to save his country's system.

Meanwhile, the United States now faced a new set of foreign policy challenges, ranging from the threat posed by "loose nukes" to worrying about failed states and ethnic conflict, terrorism, climate change, and pandemic diseases. Not least among the concerns was how to convince Americans who sacrificed so much blood and treasure containing the Soviet Union to remain engaged in the world now that the Cold War enemy was gone.

As they looked out at the world in 1989-90, Americans worried that they had lost their economic edge, and some were arguing that Germany and Japan were the true winners of the Cold War. Those two nations, which the Allies had destroyed in World War II, emerged under the U.S. nuclear umbrella to become major economic powers. Meanwhile, the United States was becoming mired in recession. In 1987, Paul Kennedy's treatise *Rise and Fall of the Great Powers* had spent 34 weeks on the *New York Times* bestseller list; the title was widely viewed as a harbinger of what faced an America that had become overstretched militarily and unproductive economically.[1] Against that backdrop, George H. W. Bush, who had seen his approval ratings soar to 90 percent when he led an international coalition to reverse Iraq's 1990 invasion of Kuwait, became increasingly unpopular. Fearing for their economic future and no longer believing they needed a President with expertise in national security matters, the American public elected a young, untested governor from Arkansas in November 1992.

As he prepared to enter office, Bill Clinton believed that the old national security apparatus was ill-suited to the new world. In particular, he sought to raise the prominence of economic actors in foreign policy decisionmaking. During the campaign, Clinton had declared, "I will elevate economics in foreign policy, create an Economic Security Council similar to the National Security Council, and change the culture in the State Department so that economics is no longer a poor cousin to old school diplomacy."[2]

In January 1993, Clinton did create the National Economic Council (NEC) as a body parallel to the National Security Council (NSC). While this reform appeared to solve what in fact was a long-standing national security problem (i.e., the failure to integrate economic and national security policies), it was not particularly successful in practice according to those who served on one or the other councils during the Clinton years. Probably the more important effort Clinton undertook was to raise the profile of his Treasury Secretary in foreign policy decisionmaking, but that was a function of his trust in the judgment of Robert Rubin, who left his position as head of the NEC in late 1994 to become Secretary of the Treasury and was a dominant foreign policy figure for the bulk of the Clinton presidency.

THE ROOTS OF THE PROBLEM

During the Cold War, policymakers understood in principle that international trade and finance had implications for national security, but no one worried too much about whether the government was organized effectively to integrate economic decisionmaking and national security decisionmaking. Both scholars and government officials, in fact, distinguished between high politics (nuclear issues and crisis management) and low politics (economics and the environment). International trade and finance could certainly affect perceptions of how the country was doing, but it was the "old school diplomacy," as Clinton referred to it, that would determine whether we blew up the world.

In fact, while Presidents John F. Kennedy and Lyndon Johnson had an NSC deputy oversee international economic issues, Henry Kissinger, who, along with

George F. Kennan, was considered the greatest strategist of the post-World War II period, did not bother to have an economic deputy because the issues did not interest him. Richard Nixon created the Council on International Economic Policy (CIEP) in 1971, but it was effective only during the brief period in 1973-74 when Treasury Secretary George Shultz chaired the CIEP as well. Gerald Ford's Economic Policy Board was generally regarded as highly effective, but Jimmy Carter's Economic Policy Group was less so.[3]

In the latter half of the Cold War, economic and national security policy remained largely uncoordinated, and close observers of the process complained. William Hyland, who had served in Kissinger's NSC, argued in 1980:

> . . . a bad defect in the [NSC] system is that it does not have any way of addressing international economic problems. The big economic agencies . . . are not in the NSC system, but obviously energy problems, trade, and arms sales are foreign policy issues. Every Administration tries to drag them in, usually by means of some kind of a subcommittee or a separate committee. The committee eventually runs up against some other committee. There is friction, and policies are made on a very ad hoc basis by the principal cabinet officers.[4]

Twelve years later, Harvard Professor Ernest May spoke before Congress and made the following observation:

> In the early 1980s, the greatest foreign threat was default by Mexico and Brazil. That could have brought down the American banking system. Despite good CIA analysis and energetic efforts by some NSC staffers, the question did not get on the NSC agenda for more than two years. And then, the policy issues

did not get discussed. The agencies concerned with money and banking had no natural connection with either the NSC or the intelligence community. We have no reason to suppose that agencies concerned with the new policy issues will be any more receptive.[5]

FROM BUSH TO CLINTON

That is where things stood as the Cold War ended. In the final year of the George H. W. Bush administration, two competing visions of the threats facing America emerged. The most well known is the 1992 Defense Planning Guidance (DPG), produced for Secretary of Defense Dick Cheney's Pentagon under the supervision of Undersecretary for Policy Paul Wolfowitz and leaked to the *New York Times*. Unsurprisingly, given its authorship at the Pentagon, the DPG focused on national security issues in a very traditional way. In an early draft, the DPG stated,

> Our first objective is to prevent the re-emergence of a new rival, either on the territory of the former Soviet Union or elsewhere, that poses a threat on the order of that posed formerly by the Soviet Union. This is a dominant consideration underlying the new regional defense strategy and requires that we endeavor to prevent any hostile power from dominating a region whose resources would, under consolidated control, be sufficient to generate global power.[6]

But the DPG expressed concern not just about a new Soviet Union (a challenge most people believed would come from a rising China), but also that America's friends might strengthen and challenge the position of the United States in Europe and Asia. "We must account sufficiently for the interests of the advanced industrial nations to discourage them from challenging our leadership or seeking to overturn the established political and economic order."[7]

If that is how the U.S. Government was going to view the world, then no organizational changes or new thinking would be needed. We could just prepare for the new world with the same machinery used to make national security policy in the old. But others in the government were beginning to recognize that the new world would be different.

Across the Potomac River at the Department of State, advisers to Acting Secretary Lawrence Eagleburger developed an approach later in 1992 that was quite different from that expressed by their Pentagon colleagues. Compiled in a 22-page secret memorandum to incoming Secretary of State Warren Christopher, Eagleburger's missive argued that the new security challenges were not rising powers but transnational threats. Powerful states were not the problem, wrote Eagleburger, it was disintegrating states that would now consume America's attention. "Alongside the globalization of the world economy," the memo read, "the international political system is tilting schizophrenically toward greater fragmentation." Noting the civil war in the former Yugoslavia was raging, the transition memo asserted that "our basic stake is in peaceful processes of change rather than clinging blindly to old maps . . . this is going to confront us with the dilemma of whether to take part in limited military interventions in situations which do not directly threaten our interests . . . ." And most significantly, Eagleburger argued, "The most important global challenge we face is the emergence of an increasingly interdependent and competitive global economy."[8]

This transition memo fed easily into the incoming Clinton team's worldview. One of Bill Clinton's core insights in his run for president was that in a globalizing world, we could no longer pretend that there was a domestic economy along with a separate international economy. Clinton had been heavily influenced by the book *The Work of Nations* (1991), written by his Oxford and Yale classmate, Robert Reich. "We are living through a transformation that will rearrange the politics and economics of the coming century," Reich wrote. "There will no longer be *national* products or technologies, no national corporations, no national industries. . . . Each nation's primary political task will be to cope with the centrifugal forces of the global economy which tear at the ties binding citizens together — bestowing even greater wealth on the most skilled and insightful, while consigning the less skilled to a declining standard of living."[9]

Looked at from this vantage point, foreign policy was now substantially about economic policy. The Department of the Treasury alone was not sufficient to deal with it. As Clinton had presaged in his August 1992 speech in Los Angeles, the new President wanted an organization in the White House that would parallel the National Security Council and work alongside it to manage these cross-cutting issues. The National Economic Council, headed by Wall Street financier Robert Rubin, thus came into being. According to Rubin's deputy, Bowman Cutter, White House budgetary pressures led to the idea of having an international economic staff that would report both to Rubin and to National Security Adviser Anthony Lake.[10]

If having "dual-hatted" staff members reporting to both the Assistant to the President for Economic Policy and the Assistant to the President for National

Security Affairs was supposed to ensure coordinated policy, it did not play out that way in practice. Clinton himself later touted the creation of the NEC as one of his great accomplishments, saying in 2000, "I believe that no future President will be able to have a White House that doesn't have a National Economic Council that coordinates all the various parts of the government to deal with economics."[11]

Clinton was successful in developing an economic policy that created jobs and slashed the budget deficit. But he had not created an institution that worked smoothly with its national security counterpart. Samuel "Sandy" Berger, who had served as Deputy National Security Adviser and then National Security Adviser during the Clinton years, later said, "It was always a little bit difficult to mesh gears," adding, "I don't think the NSC-NEC process worked that well."[12] Meanwhile, from the other side of the equation, Cutter complained that the international economic staff was "an orphan within the NSC" because the NSC never treated that group as a meaningful part of the staff.[13]

But Clinton's efforts involved more than just creating the NEC. Again as he presaged in his campaign speech in Los Angeles, he also raised the Department of Treasury's prominence in the conduct of foreign policy.

In the 1990s, it was not a hard sell to argue that economic issues should share the foreign policy stage with traditional national security policy. After all, it seemed that America had finally created a world without major national security threats. Wars would now be fought for purposes of humanitarian intervention, not to combat major world powers. Additionally, if the most important international challenge was, as Eagleburger had written to Christopher during the transition, the interdependent global economy, then it would make sense that American economic policy should now lie at the core of the country's foreign and national security determinations.

The economic team did play an enormous role in shaping foreign policy during the 1990s. In part, it was because of the tremendous respect the President had for Rubin and others on the economic side, such as Lawrence Summers, who by the mid-1990s became Rubin's deputy at the Treasury department and would later become Clinton's final Secretary of the Treasury (and still later Barack Obama's director of the National Economic Council).

For some on the national security side, the economic team was, at times, too prominent, giving short shrift to national security considerations. In July 1997, a run on the Thai currency led to a massive crisis as that country's foreign exchange reserves dwindled. It appeared that Thailand would require a bailout, just as Mexico had two years earlier. The national security team—Berger, Secretary of State Madeleine Albright, and Secretary of Defense William Cohen—urged the President to provide assistance to Thailand, an American military ally. But Rubin and Summers argued that the United States should allow the International Monetary Fund to take the lead, fearful of congressional opposition to bilateral assistance.

Writing later, Clinton's second term deputy national security adviser, James Steinberg, complained vociferously about what had occurred. "Many in Thailand—a U.S. treaty ally—and others in Asia questioned what that decision said about America's commitment to its friends in the region," Steinberg argued on the pages of the *Washington Post*. "It was a decision made largely through the apparatus for international economic policymaking with little input or attention being provided by the national security and foreign policy agencies."[14]

Thus if the concern in the Cold War had been that economics was the poor cousin of high-level diplomacy, now economics was trumping national security. Coordination still eluded the top policymakers, who at least recognized the problem that they were trying to address in the 1990s. Unfortunately, the new team largely brought an old national security concept with them in 2001.

ECONOMICS AND NATIONAL SECURITY AFTER 9/11

The sense that economic issues were on par with national security issues ended (at least temporarily) on September 11, 2001 (9/11). In truth, the notion ended when the George W. Bush team took office. Vice President Cheney, a former Secretary of Defense, now came to dominate the process, with help from his old colleague, the new Secretary of Defense Donald Rumsfeld. Treasury Secretary Paul O'Neill was no Bush insider, and he was soon relegated to a background role, as was the NEC. Foreign policy was once again about traditional issues: the Anti-Ballistic Missile Treaty with Russia, the looming threat from China, and the need for regime change in Iraq. Then, of course, came the horrific events of 9/11.

In response, the United States went to war in Afghanistan, and soon after launched a military campaign in Iraq. National security was again dominant as it had been during the Cold War. Yet by the end of the Bush years, it was clear that national security policymaking alone was not sufficient to ensure America's interests. Even with respect to the particular issue of counterterrorism, a core factor was the need to disrupt the financing of terrorist groups. Then came the financial crisis of 2008, threatening to create an economic meltdown that the United States had not seen since the 1930s. As Barack Obama prepared to assume the presidency, the question about the ability of the United States to coordinate its economic and national security policies had surfaced once again.

THE OBAMA ADMINISTRATION

On March 18, 2009, National Security Adviser James Jones sent a memorandum to the heads of agencies serving on the National Security Council. As William Hyland might have argued in 1980, or Ernest May in 1992, or James Steinberg in 2001, Jones suggested that "The United States must navigate an environment in which traditional organizations and means of response to global challenges may be inadequate or deficient." The memo went on, "To succeed, the United States must integrate its ability to employ all elements of national power in a cohesive manner. In order to deal with the world as it is, rather than how we wish it were, the National Security Council must be transformed to meet the realities of the new century." In that memo, Jones prescribed that the agencies represented on the NSC would have a senior person in the front office whose job would be to communicate with the NSC staff.[15]

Another step by the Obama administration to reconfigure the national security apparatus was the creation of a "cyber-czar" who would report both to the NEC and NSC. Still another step was transforming the George W. Bush administration's Strategic Economic

Dialogue with China into a Strategic and Economic Dialogue, involving both the Secretary of the Treasury and the Secretary of State rather than just the former, as had been the case under Bush Treasury Secretary Henry Paulson. Obama also appointed as Deputy National Security Adviser for International Economic Affairs his law school classmate, Michael Froman, who reports both to the heads of the NSC and NEC, in an effort to improve upon the situation that existed in both the Clinton and George W. Bush administrations.

In Steinberg's 2001 *Washington Post* article alluded to earlier, he made the case for the "increasing irrelevance of trying to pigeonhole complex policy problems as solely 'economic' or 'national security' or 'law enforcement'," complaining that "our decisionmaking apparatus fails to reflect that reality." His proposed solution was to create "a single international policy staff that spans the four basic areas: national security, international economics, international law enforcement, and science technology policy." In addition to a national security adviser and a science advisor, Steinberg suggested that the President also name an assistant for international economic affairs as well as one for counterterrorism, infrastructure protection, and international crime.[16] We don't know whether Steinberg suggested such a reorganization when he was part of the 2009 transition, but to date such reforms have not been made. Essentially, the system is structured nearly as it was in the Clinton years. As it was then, and often still is, how well the structure works will depend on personalities.

WHAT CAN BE DONE?

For decades, foreign policy elites have recognized that we need to think differently about foreign and national security policy, and particularly that we need to find a better way to integrate our economic policymaking with our national security policymaking. One problem that immediately arises is staff capacity and attention span. When it comes to international economic issues, it is not just countries that matter, but also the various nonstate actors, both private and public. Even if the White House has its act together, it may not be able to perform all the coordination necessary to manage the issues.

There is also a different type of capacity problem. The community of foreign policy experts tends not to have a lot of economic expertise. This became a huge problem in the Clinton efforts to bridge the gap. When a principal such as Rubin or Summers explained a policy prescription by emphasizing the nature of international markets, it was hard for those on the national security side to counter those arguments—these national security actors did not have the economic literacy (or reputation) to counter.

We have seen in the Obama administration an effort to address that problem by bringing people with such knowledge on board across the government. Vice President Biden created the new position of vice-presidential economic policy adviser and hired free-trade skeptic Jared Bernstein to fill it. Robert Hormats, who has decades of experience in Washington as well as the private sector, has been mentioned as the likely nominee to be Hillary Clinton's Undersecretary of State for Economics, Business, and Agricultural Affairs. These types of individuals can perform a useful role in advising their principals when international economic issues are discussed in a national security context.

Past administrations were well served when individuals with a strong economics or business background were named Secretary of State—e.g., George Shultz in the Reagan years and James Baker under George H. W. Bush had each served previously as Secretary of Treasury. But economic input and clout can become excessive. It would also be useful if those in the NEC and Treasury Department had a strong enough grounding in national security issues not to believe that all questions can be reduced to the issue of how markets are likely to respond.

CONCLUDING THOUGHTS

Fifty years ago, Bernard Brodie published the important work *Strategy in the Missile Age*. The central problem Brodie addressed was how did the nuclear age change strategic thinking? Previous strategists thought about how to fight and win wars. Brodie argued that because a nuclear war was unwinnable (and a preventive war went against America's self-image), deterrence had to become the foundation of our national security strategy.[17]

An all-out nuclear war is not a concern of today's strategists. National security strategists have to worry about a range of problems, from traditional balance-of-power questions such as the impact of the rise of Asia, to new security challenges, which include terrorism, the possession of weapons of mass destruction by failing states and nonstate actors, climate change, energy dependence, and cyber-warfare.

If Brodie were alive and writing today, would he be penning "Strategy in the Information Age"? If so, presumably he would notice that the government is still largely organized as it was during the Cold War. Steinberg recommended an international policy staff that could serve the President.[18] But we also require better interaction between the Departments of State and Treasury. Perhaps foreign service officers should be required to have stronger grounding in economics. Certainly the incentives in government should be restructured so that those who can bridge economic and national security are rewarded, whether they initially come from the economic or national security side of the house.

ENDNOTES - CHAPTER 5

1. Paul Kennedy, *Rise and Fall of the Great Powrs*, New York: Random House, 1987.

2. Governor Bill Clinton, Speech before the Los Angeles World Affairs Council, August 13, 1992.

3. Jonathan Orszag, Peter Orszag, and Laura Tyson, "The Process of Economic Policymaking During the Clinton Administration," Paper prepared for the conference on "American Economic Policy in the 1990s," Center for Business and Government, John F. Kennedy School of Government, Harvard University, June 27-30, 2001.

4. As quoted in Richard A. Best, Jr., "The National Security Council: An Organizational Assessment," Congressional Research Service Report for Congress, April 21, 2008.

5. *Ibid.*

6. "Excerpts from Pentagon's Plan: 'Prevent the Re-Emergence of a New Rival'," *New York Times*, March 8, 1992, p. 14; Patrick E. Tyler, "U.S. Strategy Plan Calls for Insuring No Rivals Develop," *New York Times*, March 8, 1992, p. 1.

7. Patrick E. Tyler, "Lone Superpower Plan: Ammunition for Critics," *New York Times*, March 10, 1992, p. A12; Patrick E. Tyler, "Senior U.S. Officials Assail Lone-Superpower Policy," *New York Times*, March 11, 1992, p. A6.

8. Derek Chollet and James Goldgeier, *America Between the Wars: From 11/9 to 9/11*, New York: PublicAffairs, 2008, pp. 47-51.

9. Robert Reich, *The Work of Nations*, New York: Vintage Books, 1991, p. 3.

10. The National Security Council Project, Oral History Roundtables, "International Economic Policymaking and the National Security Council," February 11, 1999, College Park, MD: Center for International Security Studies at Maryland, and Washington, DC: The Brookings Institution, moderated by Ivo Daalder and I. M. Destler.

11. Michael Paterniti, "Bill Clinton: The Exit Interview," *Esquire Magazine*, available from *www.mega.nu:8080/ampp/clinterview.html*.

12. Ivo H. Daalder and I. M. Destler, *In the Shadow of the Oval Office: Profiles of the National Security Advisers and the Presidents They Served — From JFK to George W. Bush*, New York: Simon & Schuster, 2009, p. 244.

13. The National Security Council Project, p. 34.

14. James Steinberg, "Foreign Policy: Time to Regroup," *Washington Post*, January 2, 2001, p. A15.

15. "The 21st Century Interagency Process," Memorandum from the National Security Adviser, March 18, 2009.

16. Steinberg, p. A15.

17. Bernard Brodie, *Strategy in the Missile Age*, Princeton, NJ: Princeton University Press, 1959.

18. Steinberg, p. A15.

CHAPTER 6

A FINE BALANCE:
THE EVOLUTION OF THE NATIONAL
SECURITY ADVISER

Andrew Preston

Within the national security bureaucracy, no role is as pivotal as the National Security Adviser's. He or she alone stands at all the pivotal points in the policymaking apparatus; it is no exaggeration to say that most information reaching the President will have first passed through the Adviser's hands. The National Security Adviser also has a unique combination of functions as both policy manager and policymaker. He or she acts as a broker of views for other administration officials — often including cabinet secretaries — and as an advocate for his or her own views. Ideally the National Security Adviser should be an "honest broker," conveying the views and positions of other presidential advisers objectively and accurately, uncolored by his own views of those of others. It is no coincidence that the term honest broker is usually used to describe the Adviser's ideal performance. Overall then, the National Security Adviser possesses an extraordinary and unrivalled authority over both policy and process in the making and implementing of U.S. foreign policy.[1]

The National Security Adviser's managerial authority stems from his or her role as the effective executive secretary of the National Security Council (NSC). The Adviser's policymaking influence stems from his or her role as the President's foremost staff member on foreign policy. The Adviser's bureaucratic stature is rooted in both of these roles, and is augmented by the fact that advisers have a policymaking staff of their own. As George Ball, Under Secretary of State in the Kennedy and Johnson administrations, once put it, the NSC staff operates as a "foreign office in microcosm," because it is comprised of a small number of policy experts with their own specialty issues (for example, arms control, terrorism, economics) or regions.[2] The NSC staff works directly for the Adviser and, through him or her, the President; staff members work for nobody else and cannot be drafted by any other department or agency, including the State or Defense Departments. They are not even subject to congressional oversight. When the President names his Adviser, confirmation by the Senate is not required.

Given the National Security Adviser's potent combination of tremendous power and independence, it is unsurprising that the position has been a source of controversy. Some advisers having used their dual role as a policy manager and formulator and have clearly not acted as honest brokers, instead using their influence and access to the President to force their own views on the national security bureaucracy, to include the secretaries of State and Defense. Others have marginalized the cabinet secretaries and their respective departments in the policymaking process. Henry Kissinger, National Security Adviser to Richard Nixon, often kept Secretary of State William Rogers completely in the dark about policymaking, even in areas that were clearly within the State Department's traditional or constitutional jurisdiction. Kissinger had more limited success in marginalizing the Secretaries of Defense with whom he worked, Melvin Laird, James Schlesinger, and Donald Rumsfeld, only because they were much savvier and tougher than the hapless Rogers.[3] While no other Adviser has acted with as much independence or impudence as Kissinger, several have alienated their cabinet colleagues and even had a hand in their ouster. Walt Rostow, National Security Adviser to Lyndon Johnson, helped marginalize Secretary of Defense Robert McNamara, while Zbigniew Brzezinski, Jimmy Carter's Adviser, constantly—and in the end triumphantly—battled Secretary of State Cyrus Vance for supremacy of the Carter administration's foreign policy.[4]

Such abuses have led many commentators to propose a new set of rules for the NSC system. Calls for NSC reform—shorthand for reform of the National Security Adviser's role and the functions of the NSC staff—usually occur at the beginning of every new presidency, but they are particularly voluble following foreign policy disasters. Not coincidentally, the biggest drives for change came in 1980-81, after Brzezinski's successful coup against Vance, and in 1987-89, after the Iran-Contra scandal. NSC reform did not emerge as a pressing issue following Vietnam, despite the culpability of National Security Advisers McGeorge Bundy and Walt Rostow in Vietnam policymaking, probably because their successor, Kissinger, was seen to have engineered U.S. withdrawal; moreover, Kissinger was one of the only Nixon administration officials not to have been tainted by the Watergate scandal.

In 2008-09, following the frustrations attending the U.S. invasion and occupation of Iraq, calls for NSC reform emerged yet again. President Barack Obama made it a central part of his national security proposals. However, the problem this time was not an Adviser who had grasped too much power, but too little. Following an emerging consensus, Obama sought a

National Security Adviser who would prevent bureaucratic power struggles and ideological rifts from distracting policymakers from their proper tasks. Failure to do so was thought to be Condoleezza Rice's cardinal sin as George W. Bush's Adviser.[5] Some advocates of reform, moreover, called for congressional confirmation of White House officials, such as the National Security Adviser, a change that would almost certainly require a constitutional amendment.[6]

In an effort to address these perceived shortcomings, Obama chose James L. Jones as his National Security Adviser.[7] Jones was close to Republicans as well as Democrats, including Republican presidential candidate John McCain, and had earned widespread respect throughout Washington for his bipartisanship and his military service. As a four-star Marine Corps general, Jones possessed not only undoubted expertise, but also an air of gravitas that was bound to earn him the respect of foreign policymakers in the Obama administration and lawmakers on Capitol Hill. Previous military commanders, such as Colin Powell and Brent Scowcroft, had enjoyed notable success as National Security Adviser. In short, Jones seemed to embody all the qualities one would expect from an "honest broker."

Yet thus far, neither Obama nor Jones, nor anybody else for that matter, has embarked upon serious, substantive NSC reform. Jones announced he would initiate a new policy of administration cooperation through interagency coordination, but as William Inboden — an NSC staffer in the George W. Bush administration — pointed out on his blog, this meant operating much as every Adviser had done since 1989.[8] To observers of the NSC system, especially of the role of the National Security Adviser, this should come as no surprise. Simply put, the system works. As it is currently set up, the NSC is strikingly similar to the original prototype, styled by McGeorge Bundy in the early 1960s. To be sure, the NSC system has changed since then—but not by much. When it has changed, as it did with Brent Scowcroft under President George H. W. Bush, reformers have simply refined the existing system and returned it to the fundamentals first established by Bundy. This is as it should be, for with few exceptions, the National Security Adviser and NSC staff have generally served their Presidents well. Moreover, any changes beyond refinements of the existing system will threaten to neutralize the Adviser's policymaking role. In a globalized world of complex, interconnected threats and interests, when the lines between domestic and foreign affairs are blurred, the President needs independent, flexible advice more than ever. It is the National Security Adviser and NSC staff who serve this role.

The National Security Adviser is therefore a Cold War innovation that has proven adept at confronting the globalized challenges of the post-Cold War world. As a brief history of its evolution illustrates, the NSC system long ago reached a natural equilibrium that can be upset only by a lack of presidential oversight and involvement. A severe, destabilizing series of institutional crises nearly crippled the NSC system from the late 1970s to the Iran-Contra scandal of 1986-87. Since then, despite two subsequent—though also less serious—crises of institutional authority in 1993-94 and 2002-04, the system has performed to a high standard.

In January 1961, John F. Kennedy assumed the presidency determined to be his own Secretary of State. Reacting to perceived impediments under his predecessor, Dwight D. Eisenhower, Kennedy wanted to be free of two roadblocks obstructing presidential control of foreign policy: a powerful Secretary of State, and a cumbersome bureaucracy. Regarding the former, the notion that Secretary of State John Foster Dulles had really been in charge of Eisenhower's foreign policy was, we now know, largely a myth, but at the time it was a powerful subtext accepted as fact. In choosing Dean Rusk as his own Secretary of State, Kennedy got precisely what he wanted: a loyal and pliant chief diplomat who would unquestioningly implement the White House's foreign policy, not Foggy Bottom's.[9]

However, the second problem—a large and unwieldy bureaucracy centered mainly within the National Security Council (NSC) system—proved to be trickier, for Kennedy could not simply do away with all of Eisenhower's sprawling national security policymaking structure.[10] Besides, Kennedy did not want to eliminate the NSC system entirely—instead, he wanted to make it more flexible and responsive to the President's needs. Kennedy's solution was to take the existing NSC staff, a purely administrative body that did not actually make or even propose foreign policy, and re-create it as a smaller, more agile policymaking group. Kennedy abolished the formal groups of the Eisenhower system, kept its basics—the NSC Special Assistant and his staff—and transformed them into a powerful, substantive unit.

To fulfill this radical change in the mechanics of U.S. foreign policymaking—probably the most important and enduring since the passage of the National Security Act in 1947—President Kennedy turned to McGeorge Bundy, a professor of government and college dean at Harvard. Bundy was an ideal choice: at

Harvard, he had functioned as both teacher and administrator—and by all accounts was supremely successful at both. He was both thinker and doer, intellectual and bureaucrat. When he moved from Cambridge to Washington, Bundy essentially became the dean of the White House, or at least of its foreign policy. He advised on policy matters and ensured they were implemented. He controlled information to and from the Oval Office and acted as President Kennedy's gatekeeper when people, both inside the administration and out, sought a presidential meeting. To assist him, Bundy empowered the NSC staff that worked for him, transforming members from mere clerks into dynamic policymakers. As President Kennedy observed, Bundy had built himself a powerful but flexible organization. He had created, with JFK's evident approval, a "little State Department."[11] Though previous Presidents had appointed NSC executive secretaries—awkwardly known as the Special Assistant to the President for National Security Affairs—Bundy in effect became the first National Security Adviser as we know it today. He was the first powerful Adviser, and the first to operate as both formulator and administrator of foreign policy.

Bundy also continued serving as the NSC's—and thus as the President's—manager of the foreign policy process. He marshaled views and policy options generated by the various executive departments and agencies and forwarded them to the President. He also acted as an intermediary between federal departments and agencies, disseminating information among them so that everyone knew where everyone else stood on a particular issue. He brought together high-level opponents—usually at the principals level, but sometimes at the deputies level. This was the honest broker role, and, by most accounts, Bundy played it well. He ensured that Presidents Kennedy and Johnson received conflicting information and opinions, and heard intelligence that ran contrary to his own views. Not everyone was satisfied with Bundy's performance. His abrasive manner and unwillingness to suffer fools — or anybody who fell short of his own formidable intellect, for that matter — caused some resentment. But even his adversaries on policy matters conceded that Bundy played fair. George Ball, the most prominent dove on Vietnam within the Johnson administration and a regular foil to Bundy, admitted that as National Security Adviser, Bundy played "a strong hand in formulating our foreign policy with only a minimum of friction with the State Department."[12] As described in a classic example from Leslie Gelb and Richard Betts's *The Irony of Vietnam: The System Worked* (1979), the Vietnam War disaster occurred not because of a failure of process, but because of a failure of policy. Poor and entirely preventable policy decisions based on bad judgment, rather than a dysfunctional process, led to war in Vietnam.[13]

But while Bundy retained the National Security Adviser's managerial functions from the Truman and Eisenhower administrations, he was also responsible for three major, substantive innovations that continue to serve as the bases for the Adviser's policy importance and bureaucratic clout.[14] First, though he continued to manage policymaking as an honest broker, Bundy became a policy advocate as well. This required a delicate balancing act, and on the whole Bundy pulled it off. Even on Vietnam, regarding which he held strong views against which there was a great deal of dissent, he mobilized vigorously against doves in the State Department, Congress, the news media, and foreign governments openly but without deliberately distorting their views.[15] To be sure, he would often present dissenting opinions to the President under a covering memo that took issue with those opinions. But he almost always acknowledged the existence of dissenting views and ensured that the President knew their substance.

Bundy's second major innovation emerged from the first: since he was now a policy advocate, it was logical for him to become a policy*maker*. Bundy, then, did not merely advocate policy options proposed by others but devised them himself. He became an independent source of policy advice for the President, and often sent such advice to the cabinet secretaries. Indeed, some of the most significant programs of the Vietnam War began under Bundy's charge in the NSC system, including the bombing program of "sustained reprisal" — soon to become famous under the codename Operation ROLLING THUNDER.[16] Sometimes, he was even charged with helping to implement policy. As such, he was the first National Security Adviser to travel alone on diplomatic missions abroad, or to lead an overseas mission. Relatedly, he was also the first to engage with the news media, often being quoted in major newspapers and appearing on television. He was even featured on the cover of *Newsweek* in 1963 and *Time* in 1965.[17] Such national and international visibility was a sharp contrast with the deliberate anonymity cultivated by Eisenhower's advisers.

Bundy's third significant innovation was the creation of a "foreign office in microcosm," JFK's prized "little State Department." Bundy was not the only new policy advocate on the national security scene. The NSC staff, previously mere clerks processing the paperwork of others, also began to generate their own recommendations in 1961. Many NSC staffers during the Bundy era, such as Walt Rostow, Carl Kaysen, Michael Forrestal, Robert Komer, and Francis Bator, had direct access to the President, a privilege enjoyed by very few others outside the NSC. Bundy and the NSC essentially acted as the President's private foreign policy think tank, offering him a source of advice, reports, and recommendations independent of the Departments of State, Defense, and the Treasury. Bundy's group offered advice on military policy, too, at times arguing with the Joint Chiefs of Staff and regional commanders about troop deployments, bombing strategies, and even battlefield tactics. As Bundy reported to Senator Henry M. Jackson, Chair of the Senate Subcommittee on National Policy Machinery, in September 1961:

> We have deliberately rubbed out the distinction between planning and operation which governed the administrative structure of the NSC staff in the last Administration.... [I]t seems to us best that the NSC staff, which is essentially a Presidential instrument, should be composed of men who can serve equally well in the process of planning and in that of operational follow up.[18]

Bundy told an interviewer:

> [Knowing exactly what the President wants is a job] only the White House staff can do. We're just going to know better than the guys in the [State] Department...what's on the President's mind, what kind of stuff he will like and what he doesn't like. That is what we do for a living, and they do a lot of other things for a living.[19]

When Bundy left Washington in March 1966 to head the Ford Foundation in New York, he reflected on the changes he had wrought. "The NSC existed in some form before I got here, and it will exist in some form after I go," he told a reporter from *Newsweek*. "But whether we have written in water, sand, or stone, I really can't say."[20] For once, the famously self-confident Bundy was being unduly modest. He had rewritten the rules mostly in stone—soft stone, to be sure, which his successors could shape in slightly different ways to suit their own needs and circumstances, but his innovations became permanent nonetheless. Since 1966, virtually every National Security Adviser has functioned within the institutional parameters Bundy had established.

Since Bundy left government service, every President—including Lyndon Johnson, the President Bundy served when he resigned—has pledged to reform the NSC system. That same year, in fact, Johnson commissioned Maxwell Taylor, a retired General and former Chairman of the Joint Chiefs, to report on ways the NSC could be improved. Taylor recommended curbing the National Security Adviser's powers, especially those of the NSC staff, and augmenting those of the State Department by placing its officers in charge of interdepartmental agencies.[21] Johnson, however, ignored the Taylor Plan and instead appointed a successor to Bundy, Walt Rostow, who was very much in the same mold.

Even Nixon and Kissinger, who radically centralized policymaking in the White House—indeed, largely in their own hands—created an elaborate policymaking structure within the NSC that was hierarchical, orderly, and consensual. Like the Taylor Plan, Kissinger's new NSC system was supposed to foster cooperation by establishing interagency committees that would coordinate the administration's foreign policy; at the top was the Washington Special Actions Group (WSAG).[22] But this was true only in theory, for not long afterwards Nixon and Kissinger decided to ignore WSAG. Though WSAG produced fine studies of the various problems bedeviling U.S. foreign policy, Nixon and Kissinger disliked and distrusted such broad-based endeavors, and instead formulated national security policy largely on their own, with the connivance of a select few on the NSC staff.

As Kissinger's actions demonstrated, the risk of granting the National Security Adviser flexibility and authority is that the federal departments charged with managing national security policy will become marginalized or ignored. In particular, the NSC's growth has come at the expense of the State Department, and at times the Adviser's stature has eclipsed even that of the Secretary of State. This was certainly the case when Kissinger was National Security Adviser — that is, of course, until he himself was appointed Secretary of State, becoming the first and only individual ever to hold both posts simultaneously. It was also the case during the Carter administration, when National Security Adviser Brzezinski and Secretary of State Vance waged an intense bureaucratic civil war which Brzezinski eventually won. Vance resigned in 1980 in protest over Carter's decision to launch a military rescue mission to free American hostages in Tehran, a decision that Vance opposed but Brzezinski had approved behind the Secretary's back. The mission failed, marking it as a failure of both process and policy. This aptly served as a symbol for Carter's foreign policy in general.[23]

By 1980, most foreign policy observers, inside government and out, felt that Brzezinski had gone too far, and that he exemplified all that was wrong with an

NSC system that had spun wildly out of control. In the 20 years since Bundy's re-creation of the position under Kennedy, the executive branch had seen four very powerful Advisers (Bundy, Rostow, Kissinger, and Brzezinski) and four Secretaries of State who were either weak (Rusk and Rogers), outmaneuvered (Vance), or peripheral (Edmund Muskie, who served for the brief period between Vance's resignation and Carter's departure from office). Though Bundy was an effective manager, the only time the system seemed to work in true perfect harmony was the period between 1973 and 1977, when Kissinger served as Secretary of State and was either National Security Adviser himself or Secretary of State and thus powerful enough not to have to worry about a rival in the NSC.

When Ronald Reagan became President in 1981, he vowed to clean up the foreign policymaking process by reducing the NSC's authority and appointing a very strong, autonomous person as Secretary of State, Alexander Haig. Reagan wanted to return to the principles of the Eisenhower administration, when the National Security Adviser managed the foreign policy paper trail, kept the President and the cabinet fully briefed, and maintained an eye on whether the President's decisions were being faithfully and efficiently implemented. Yet Reagan's best intentions only created an even greater nightmare of policymaking that nearly resulted in his impeachment. The problem was that Reagan was no Eisenhower: he was not familiar with a hierarchical decisionmaking structure, did not possess a command mentality, and did not establish clear boundaries for his officials. Ironically, the internecine strife that had crippled the Carter administration's diplomacy actually increased, and even intensified, in the Reagan administration. Six National Security Advisers served under Reagan, easily a record; since 1961, the total for all other Presidents, including Obama, is only 11. This soft touch and long leash, reflecting an absence of authority, allowed a bitter feud between Secretary of State George Shultz and Secretary of Defense Caspar Weinberger to rage wildly out of control. Even more important, Reagan's lack of oversight and failure to provide direction emboldened two of his Advisers, Robert McFarlane and John Poindexter, to secretly sell weapons to Iran and illegally supply weapons to anti-communist Nicaraguan rebels. When the plot, now known as Iran-Contra, came to light, several members of the NSC staff were convicted of breaking the law. Politically, Reagan was able to avoid impeachment proceedings only by claiming total ignorance of the scheme, which only made him appear incompetent and out of touch.[24]

The totally dysfunctional nature of the Reagan administration's foreign policymaking process brought the NSC system to its knees. Yet few suggested getting rid of it completely. Instead, the system essentially corrected itself by pulling back from the brink of bureaucratic anarchy. It did so by returning to the best of Bundy's original principles and refining them to suit the modern presidency. The Tower Commission investigation of Iran-Contra, led by former Senator John Tower, contributed some of the ideas for modest reform. Leading the way in their implementation were the next three National Security Advisers. Two of them, Frank Carlucci and Colin Powell, each served for roughly a year and restored a balance between policy management and policymaking. They positioned themselves as pivots of the Reagan administration, with information flowing to and from the White House through them. They remained policy advocates but did less implementation and none of the freewheeling common to earlier periods of the Reagan presidency.[25]

But it was their successor, under President George H. W. Bush, who solidified the return to normalcy and enhanced the NSC system by instituting sensible reforms of his own. Historians of the NSC are virtually unanimous in their praise of Brent Scowcroft's tenure as National Security Adviser. It helped that Scowcroft was personally close to Bush; when Scowcroft spoke, few doubted that he also spoke for the President. It also helped that Scowcroft knew the NSC system intimately—after all, he had already been National Security Adviser, under President Gerald Ford, and had served on the Tower Commission. Scowcroft also established a good working relationship with Secretary of State James A. Baker and Secretary of Defense Dick Cheney. Scowcroft was generally fair in acting as the President's gatekeeper on foreign policy, yet he also possessed strong views of his own and at times, such as during Operations DESERT SHIELD and DESERT STORM in the Persian Gulf, acted as an especially committed policy advocate. Most important, Scowcroft smoothed relations among departments and agencies by instituting several interagency working groups that would keep lines of communication open and forestall bureaucratic turf wars that resulted from the hoarding of information. Chief among these groups were the Principals Committee, which Scowcroft himself chaired, and the Deputies Committee, which his own deputy, Robert Gates, chaired. Overall, though his system did not always function smoothly, Scowcroft acted as an effective manager and advocate by integrating his own views within a larger, more coordinated network.[26]

Since 1993, when Bush left office, the basics of the Scowcroft operation have remained a constant feature of the NSC. Presidents Bill Clinton, George W. Bush, and Barack Obama and their Advisers have tinkered with the NSC system at the margins but left its basic features unaltered. There have been two periods when the balance between management and advocacy tilted too strongly to one side or the other, and in both cases the President and the National Security Adviser recognized the fault and moved to restore a proper working equilibrium. In 1993, to take one example, Anthony Lake focused too narrowly on management of the process at the expense of advocacy or implementation, and Clinton's foreign policy floundered aimlessly as a result.[27] To take another example, between 2002 and 2004 Condoleezza Rice concentrated on policy advocacy — acting especially as the President's advocate — and even engaged in partisan political campaigning. The result of her neglect of process was an absence of authority or oversight at the center of the Bush administration, allowing other principal players — Vice President Cheney and Secretary of Defense Donald Rumsfeld in particular — to dominate the process and enforce their own views. It was only after the disastrous consequences of the occupation of Iraq had become fully apparent that Bush, Rice, and her successor Stephen Hadley — one of the Tower Commission's lawyers — brought the emphasis between advocacy and process back into a proper balance.[28]

It is obvious why Presidents Reagan, Clinton, and George W. Bush changed their approach to the NSC: when it did not function well, their foreign policy suffered, and with it their presidency; when it functioned well, foreign policy performed well and ceased to be a source of crippling controversy. It was thus in the

President's own best interest to maintain a smoothly working NSC.

The question, however, remains: does the NSC system need renewed reformation? There is no doubt that the National Security Adviser is an important position and should remain in the structure. In the recent past, some observers have called for a return to the Eisenhower NSC system, in which the National Security Adviser acted as the NSC's executive secretary and did not advocate, let alone make, foreign policy.[29] It was indeed an ideal system for a widely revered and respected five-star general who had orchestrated the Normandy invasion in World War II and was accustomed to strict organizational hierarchies. Yet even if we grant that the Eisenhower NSC system is, in theory, the ideal system, it is implausible to make it the standard in the post-Bundy age. Eisenhower's time has simply passed.

Bundy showed what was possible under a powerful National Security Adviser; and most of his successors, especially Scowcroft, have demonstrated their utility in a world of increasing complexity and interconnectedness. Moreover, officials in Washington, from Congress to the White House to the State and Defense Departments, have grown comfortable with the degree of Adviser authority enabling the incumbent to make policy as well as manage it. Expecting Presidents to return to the more orderly structure of the Eisenhower era is thus as unwise as it is unfeasible. Tellingly, on assuming office, Adviser James Jones promised to do less policymaking and more policy managing. Instead, he experienced irrelevance and marginalization—and, in some quarters, derision—as it became clear that his more managerial approach had only excluded him from the inner circles of foreign policymaking.[30]

Trouble has generally occurred under two particular situations: (1) when the President has delegated excessive authority to the National Security Adviser, as Nixon did with Kissinger, and Carter with Brzezinski; and (2) when the President has failed to impose his authority on the foreign policy process at all, which occurred under Reagan and George W. Bush. Though both scenarios are problematic, the second — a lack of any presidential authority or direction — has been much more damaging, for it created conditions of anarchy and confusion within the executive. The Iran-Contra scandal and the failings of the occupation of Iraq were direct results of an absence of presidential control. Problems arise when the President vests too much power in the NSC, but such problems can partly — or sometimes totally — be compensated for if the National Security Adviser pursues and implements a successful foreign policy, as Kissinger did under Nixon. Such instances of success with a too powerful NSC are rare, and even in Kissinger's case serious problems arose that generated controversy and, completely apart from the Watergate scandal, raised profound questions of whether the Nixon administration — that is, President Nixon and Advisor Kissinger — acted unconstitutionally. At several moments under Presidents Nixon and Carter, the State Department in particular suffered from an overweeningly ambitious National Security Adviser and staff.

The solution, then, lies not in an excessive delegation of presidential power to (or appropriation of power by) the National Security Adviser, but a sensible diffusion of power within a presidency that positions the Adviser at the center of managing foreign policy on the President's behalf. Among National Security Advisers, the most successful managers of foreign policy have followed this course, from McGeorge Bundy to Stephen Hadley to Brent Scowcroft, unquestionably the most effective Adviser ever to hold the position.

Yet efforts to reform the NSC remain, especially temptations to more narrowly define the National Security Adviser's role. If would-be reformers within Congress decide that statutory changes to the NSC system are necessary, they should keep in mind that the role of the National Security Adviser has evolved naturally over time, since 1961, in response to both success and failure. It has discarded its worst abuses and excesses and enhanced its best features. Moreover, it has persevered in an exceedingly hostile and notoriously unforgiving bureaucratic environment to become an indispensable instrument of U.S. foreign policy, and it will continue to evolve, as it should. However, it should be left to do so largely without a Congress that legislatively imposes rigid structures or practices upon a system that thrives on flexibility.

ENDNOTES - CHAPTER 6

1. See, for example, John P. Burke, *Honest Broker? The National Security Advisor and Presidential Decision Making*, College Station: Texas A&M University Press, 2009.

2. George Ball, *The Past Has Another Pattern: Memoirs*, New York: W. W. Norton, 1982, p. 172.

3. A vast number of books and articles have been written about Kissinger's diplomacy—much of it by Kissinger himself. For an excellent portrait of his role as National Security Adviser, see Jussi Hanhimäki, *The Flawed Architect: Henry Kissinger and American Foreign Policy*, New York: Oxford University Press, 2004.

4. On Rostow, see David Milne, *America's Rasputin: Walt Rostow and the Vietnam War*, New York: Hill and Wang, 2008. On

Brzezinski, see Gerry Argyris Andrianopoulos, *Kissinger and Brzezinski: The NSC and the Struggle for Control of US National Security Policy*, London, UK: Macmillan, 1991.

5. Gordon Adams, "Obama's Test: Bringing Order to the National Security Policy Process," *Bulletin of the Atomic Scientists*, January 26, 2009, available from *www.thebulletin.org/web-edition/ columnists/gordon-adams/obamas-test-bringing-order-to-the-national-security-policy-proce*; and Karen DeYoung, "Obama's NSC Will Get New Power," *Washington Post*, February 8, 2009, p. A1.

6. Bruce Ackerman, "A Role for Congress to Reclaim," *Washington Post*, March 11, 2009, p. A15.

7. Helene Cooper, "National Security Pick: From a Marine to a Mediator," *New York Times*, November 29, 2008.

8. Will Inboden, "James Jones Fires a Shot Over the Bow," February 10, 2009, available from *shadow.foreignpolicy.com/ posts/2009/02/10/james_jones_fires_a_shot_over_the_bow*.

9. For the classic assessment of Eisenhower as the chief policymaker of the 1950s, and not Dulles or anyone else, see Fred I. Greenstein, *The Hidden-Hand Presidency: Eisenhower as Leader*, New York: Basic Books, 1982. On Rusk, see Thomas W. Zeiler, *Dean Rusk: Defending the American Mission Abroad*, Wilmington, DE: Scholarly Resources, 1999.

10. On the Eisenhower administration's policymaking structure, see Robert R. Bowie and Richard H. Immerman, *Waging Peace: How Eisenhower Shaped an Enduring Cold War Strategy*, New York: Oxford University Press, 1998, pp. 83-95.

11. Kennedy, quoted in Pierre Salinger, *With Kennedy*, New York: Doubleday, 1966, p. 68. On these changes and their importance, see Andrew Preston, "The Little State Department: McGeorge Bundy and the National Security Council Staff, 1961-65," *Presidential Studies Quarterly*, Vol. 31, No. 4, December 2001, pp. 635-659. On Bundy's performance as National Security Adviser, see Kai Bird, *The Color of Truth: McGeorge Bundy and William Bundy — Brothers in Arms*, New York: Simon & Schuster, 1998; Andrew Preston, *The War Council: McGeorge Bundy, the NSC, and*

146

Vietnam, Cambridge, MA: Harvard University Press, 2006; and Gordon Goldstein, *Lessons in Disaster: McGeorge Bundy and the Path to War in Vietnam*, New York: Times Books, 2008.

12. Ball, pp. 172-73.

13. Leslie H. Gelb, with Richard K. Betts, *The Irony of Vietnam: The System Worked*, Washington, DC: Brookings Institution Press, 1979.

14. Except where noted, the three changes discussed in the following paragraphs are examined in greater detail in Preston, "The Little State Department."

15. This is a central theme of Preston, *The War Council*.

16. *Ibid.*, pp. 167-190.

17. "JFK's McGeorge Bundy: Cool Head for the Cold War," *Newsweek*, March 4, 1963; "The Crucial Choice: U.S. Foreign Policy in Action," *Time*, June 25, 1965.

18. Quoted in Preston, "The Little State Department," p. 645.

19. *Ibid.*

20. Quoted in Preston, *The War Council*, p. 247.

21. Cody M. Brown, *The National Security Council: A Legal History of the President's Most Powerful Advisers*, Washington, DC: Project on National Security Reform, 2008, pp. 30-31, available from *www. pnsr.org/data/images/the%20national%20security%20council.pdf*.

22. Asaf Siniver, *Nixon, Kissinger, and U.S. Foreign Policy Making: The Machinery of Crisis*, Cambridge, MA: Cambridge University Press, 2008, pp. 64-70.

23. On the Brzezinski-Vance feud and its effects, see John Prados, *Keepers of the Keys: A History of the National Security Council from Truman to Bush*, New York: Morrow, 1991, pp. 379-445.

24. For an excellent account, see Ivo H. Daalder and I. M.

Destler, *In the Shadow of the Oval Office: Profiles of the National Security Advisers and the Presidents They Served — From JFK to George W. Bush*, New York: Simon & Schuster, 2009, pp. 127-162.

25. *Ibid.*, pp. 162-167.

26. David Rothkopf, *Running the World: The Inside Story of the National Security Council and the Architects of American Power*, New York: PublicAffairs, 2005, pp. 266-269.

27. Daalder and Destler, pp. 214-235.

28. On the loss of balance under Rice, see Bob Woodward, *Plan of Attack*, New York: Simon & Schuster, 2004, pp. 414-415; and Elisabeth Bumiller, *Condoleezza Rice: An American Life*, New York: Random House, 2007, pp. 217-223. On its restoration under Hadley, see Daalder and Destler, pp. 292-298.

29. Fred I. Greenstein and Richard H. Immerman, "Effective National Security Advising: Recovering the Eisenhower Legacy," *Political Science Quarterly*, Vol. 115, No. 3, Autumn 2000, pp. 335-345.

30. Helene Cooper, "National Security Adviser Tries Quieter Approach," *New York Times*, May 7, 2009; Jonathan Miller and Ben Smith, "Reporters Have a Jones for NSC Profiles," *Politico*, May 8, 2009, available from *www.politico.com/news/stories/0509/22251.html*.

CHAPTER 7

LEADING THE NEXT PHASE OF HOMELAND SECURITY INTELLIGENCE: PROVIDING BETTER DEFINITIONS, ROLES, AND PROTECTIONS

Geoffrey S. French[1]

The terrorist attacks of September 11, 2001 (9/11), exposed major gaps in the collection, exchange, and synthesis of intelligence that may otherwise have prevented them. In its assessment of that intelligence failure, the National Commission on Terrorist Attacks upon the United States (the 9/11 Commission) referred not to a breakdown in foreign intelligence or domestic intelligence, but to a void that existed between the two spheres.[2] This sense of a void rather than a simple malfunction of an existing apparatus partially explains the sheer number of security information-sharing initiatives that have been launched since 2001. Indeed, reform of government intelligence and security activities, authorities, and organizations has been constant from 2001 to the present, typically driven by a sense of urgency derived from the initial shock of the attacks. Major legislation has included:

- The Uniting and Strengthening America by Providing Appropriate Tools Required to Intercept and Obstruct Terrorism (USA PATRIOT) Act of 2001,
- Homeland Security Act of 2002,
- Intelligence Reform and Terrorism Prevention Act of 2004 (IRTPA), and
- Implementing Recommendations of the 9/11 Act.

Other reforms included the establishment of the U.S. Department of Homeland Security (DHS) and the Terrorism Threat Integration Center (TTIC), later renamed the National Counterterrorism Center (NCTC), and the addition of resources to existing counterterrorism missions in the U.S. Department of Defense (DoD) and civilian agencies. The state and local levels of government, as well as institutions, shifted resources to the counterterrorism efforts as well.

The first phase of reform, in other words, sought to fill the void in the generation and exchange of intelligence pertinent to homeland security by a number of means; in retrospect, filling it seems to have been a higher priority than creating a coherent approach to address the issue of homeland security intelligence (HSINT). Kate Martin, director of the Center for National Security Studies, summarized the situation succinctly in her testimony before Congress in 2009: "There has also been a proliferation of agencies and entities with domestic intelligence responsibilities, although it is not clear that such arrangement was a deliberate effort to create redundancy or just an accident resulting from so many different initiatives by different actors."[3]

A change in administration is an artificial marker of the passing of time, but it does often provide a useful occasion to pause and reexamine governmental approaches and the need for reform. The issue of HSINT is certainly in need of such a review. Even a basic review, in this case, reveals an inability to define HSINT, leading to obvious problematic implications for the information-sharing activities surrounding it. More importantly, collecting intelligence without protecting it from the very adversaries it is meant to address creates a critical vulnerability that threatens

150

to destabilize the partnerships established to date. A thorough review exposes an emerging need for a new discipline: counterintelligence for homeland security.

DEFINING HOMELAND SECURITY INTELLIGENCE

Given the importance imputed to homeland security since 2001 and the crucial role of information exchange in the success of the many organizations involved in the spectrum of homeland security–related activities, one would think that finding the definition of HSINT is easy. Indeed, there have been multiple attempts to find a definition for HSINT over the past few months. In 2009, the Congressional Research Service published a thorough review of perspectives on HSINT, highlighting the areas of agreement and difference, and Congress has held hearings on its roles and limitations, Yet, no single authoritative definition or consensus has been found.[4]

The first potential source for such a definition is from DHS itself. DHS does not have a formal definition, however. The most recent Chief Intelligence Officer for DHS, Charles Allen, testified on the topic of HSINT on several occasions, describing it succinctly (if informally): the "essence of what constitutes homeland security intelligence is a simple concept — threats to the U.S. Homeland." HSINT, in this view, is the "unique mission" of DHS in support of the "Secretary and the Department; [its] partners at the state, local, and tribal levels, and in the private sector; and in the Intelligence Community."[5] Although one can argue whether HSINT belongs uniquely to DHS, the department and its mission are a focal point for HSINT activities and therefore a useful starting point for framing the definition.

Unfortunately, the legal foundation for DHS also lacks a formal definition. The Homeland Security Act of 2002, (Public Law 107-296, November 23, 2002) defines homeland security *information* as:

> Any information that relates to the threat of terrorist activity and the ability to prevent it, as well as information that would improve the response to terrorist activity or the identification or investigation of a suspected terrorist or terrorist organization.

If DHS can be considered a microcosm of the homeland security effort, however, this definition does not capture the other major threats that the department faces, such as organized criminal groups, drug-trafficking organizations, transnational gangs, and alien-smuggling rings. Terrorism—although the primary impetus for the creation of DHS and the basis of HSINT—does not suffice to define the boundaries of HSINT.

Similarly, the term "domestic intelligence" does not adequately bound the issues of homeland security. Although DHS's focus is on the application of intelligence to domestic issues, the intelligence itself focuses more often than not on transnational entities. There are certainly domestic terrorist groups that warrant observation by the law enforcement community, but international terrorist groups, criminal organizations, and transnational gangs require the fusion of domestic intelligence with foreign intelligence.

This complexity highlights the inherent difference between the traditional role of the intelligence community and the new role required of DHS and the HSINT community. For military intelligence, the military is both a collector and the primary consumer.

Foreign intelligence has many more applications and consumers, but there is still a relatively limited group needing to receive intelligence reports or analysis, and there are clear rules for how to share and protect such information. In contrast, potential HSINT consumers include: the law enforcement community; federal, state, local, and tribal governments; owners and operators of critical infrastructure; and the public. Similarly, those very same consumers may also be collectors. Citizens or operators of critical infrastructure may be in a position to observe and report suspicious activity or other anomalous behavior that is pertinent to combating a criminal organization, a gang, or a terrorist group. This is not to argue for a police state mentality, with citizens expected to inform on neighbors and friends. It is merely to note that important tips about criminal and terrorist groups often come from ordinary citizens and organizations and not from formal intelligence collection activities. (Some have even argued that the private sector can contribute to the entire intelligence cycle, including the generation of intelligence requirements.[6]) HSINT, in other words, is unique in that its success depends not on retaining the information within a small, closed community, but rather sharing it with very broad segments of society.

The challenge, therefore, is to draw proper boundaries, if any, for the concept of HSINT. The HSINT community has not overcome this obstacle yet. For lack of a formal definition, the term "homeland security intelligence" as used in this chapter is understood to mean intelligence applied to protect against domestic and transnational threats to critical infrastructure and urban security.

NEW FRAMEWORKS FOR INFORMATION SHARING

The erstwhile lack of a definition for HSINT has led directly to other ambiguities that prevent the HSINT community from effectively collecting, sharing, and analyzing information. First, it confines the definition of the HSINT community so as to exclude the assemblage of federal agencies, state and local law enforcement, and private partners that participate on a consistent or ad hoc basis. It thereby prevents true scope and clarity, for example, on the role of DHS in comparison with the Federal Bureau of Investigation, which has outreach programs to the private sector, including critical infrastructure, and a lead role in law enforcement and counterintelligence — or with NCTC, which is intended to centralize analysis of international terrorism and has some outreach to state and local law enforcement. In some ways, the sheer number of federal entities, information-sharing partnerships, systems, and databases testifies not to the effectiveness of the current combined effort, but to its incoherence.

Second, the lack of definition prevents a true evaluation of the effectiveness of HSINT. When the goal of information sharing itself cannot be identified, the only possible metrics are the availability of information-sharing mechanisms or technologies, or meaningless counts of the number of reports or megabytes of data exchanged. In the DHS 5-year report on progress in implementing recommendations from the 9/11 Commission, for example, it discusses information-sharing explicitly only in terms of the easily quantifiable numbers of state and local fusion centers, the dollar amount of grant allocations to support information-sharing, and the increasing availability of certain information-sharing networks.[7] A survey published in 2009, reveals the effects of such a statistics-based approach, concluding that the measurement of information sharing through the examination of the availability of systems leads to a neglect of focus on the true goals of information sharing, whether in mission effectiveness or community preparedness.[8] Similarly, the March 2009 hearings before the Subcommittee on Intelligence, Information Sharing, and Terrorism Risk Assessment of the Committee on Homeland Security revealed problems not with the means of sharing information, but rather with the HSINT activities themselves: confusion over the DHS advisory system, questions over priority of security issues, and dissatisfaction with the ability to analyze suspicious activity reports.[9] The emphasis on sharing information without clear definitions of what that information is, with whom it should be shared, and common goals inevitably leads to poor decisions, investments, and outcomes.

There is a general need, therefore, for one or more frameworks that would help focus the goals of information sharing. Two such frameworks are immediately available. The first is an emphasis on threat information that supports risk-based decisionmaking. When tactical threat analysis—such as the identification of a specific terrorist cell or an active plot—is available, its application is relatively straightforward. Most HSINT, however, is more strategic in nature, providing indications of an adversary's capability or intent to pursue a course of action. Additionally, it tends to have some degree of uncertainty, often due to unreliability of the source, staleness of the information, or credibility problems. The challenge, therefore, is not typically how to share the information; fusion centers, for example, allow a city or region to integrate information from federal agencies with its own law enforcement information and reports of suspicious activity from local operators of critical infrastructure. Instead, the challenge is how to use strategic HSINT. A single report of adversary capability may indeed be valid in a vacuum, but it is not a compelling case for action without the context provided by risk analysis which aligns the threat with the vulnerability to and consequence of the adversary's actions. By using a risk framework as the basis for collecting, sharing, and re-porting threat information, fusion centers will have a way to integrate the various reports into consistent and comparative threat levels for region-specific sce-narios. A report from George Mason University de-scribes one such approach used for an assessment of the National Capital Region,[10] which may be useful as a model for other regions in that it delivered the type of information reported to be useful in community preparedness: geographically-specific intelligence about specific adversaries.[11]

The direct threat to a city or region, however, is only one aspect of the counterterrorism and broader homeland security mission. A terrorist group or gang may use one region to raise money or acquire weapons, another to recruit members, and another for communication. In this sense, an adversary can be seen as being in competition with the homeland se-curity community as a whole; obtaining the resources it needs to continue to operate puts it in confronta-tion with immigration, customs, or other law enforce-ment. To adopt a military term, the various regions of the country constitute the domestic battlespace in which the adversary operates. Capitalizing on this perspective, the second analytic framework that could help focus the goals of HSINT is the U.S. military's methodology for Intelligence Preparation of the Battlespace (IPB).[12] IPB requires analysts to understand the political, social, and economic factors affecting an adversary's operations, thus allowing the analysts to view the adversary as a dynamic actor with needs and dependencies as well as goals and objectives. It builds to an assessment of the adversary's potential courses of action and facilitates effects-based outcomes to gain a high-level perspective of how an adversary may react. If fusion centers had a better understanding of how an adversary operates in their regions, the participating agencies could more effectively counter the adversary's actions. If DHS had insight into every fusion center's activities, it would be in a position to coordinate across regions and minimize unintended consequences. In this way, the IPB methodology could help support decisionmaking at all levels and help prioritize and coordinate action by focusing it on specific desired effects on the adversary.

INTELLIGENCE AND COUNTERINTELLIGENCE

Despite the absence of formal definitions, common frameworks, clear roles, and delineated responsibilities for HSINT, many government agencies are investing heavily in time and resources to share information from investigations, interviews, informants, other human intelligence, signals intelligence, and other intelligence disciplines. This activity may have limited value due to the hindrances discussed above, but the continued engagement of state, local, and tribal governments—as well as the private sector—indicates that there is some value. A second indicator of the value of the HSINT community's information and information-sharing systems is that various adversaries have begun to exploit them.

In October 2008, for example, press reports revealed that the Sinaloa drug cartel had an informant in the U.S. embassy in Mexico City with access to information on DEA operations.[13] One such insider was able to gain information shared between the U.S. and Mexican governments on operations against organized criminal groups and drug-trafficking organizations and passed it on to the cartel. Similarly, in 2005, the target of a U.S. terrorism investigation duped Weiss Rasool, a sergeant with the Fairfax County Police, into using Rasool's access to FBI information to identify the surveillance vehicles. The target provided Rasool with the license plate numbers from cars that the target suspected were following him, which Rasool ran through an FBI database. Rasool saw that the vehicles were not registered to individuals but to a leasing company and thus likely were used for federal law enforcement. He relayed this information to the target of the investigation, tipping him to the federal surveillance and undermining the investigation.[14] This new, ill-defined, and nontraditional type of intelligence has value, in other words, not only to the HSINT community, but also to the very adversaries it is meant to combat.

As local law enforcement organizations consolidate intelligence from informants, interviews, and observations,[15] they create the possibility that a single point of vulnerability could compromise all of their informants. If they share information across regions, then one city's intelligence could be spoiled by its being compromised by another city's intelligence center. If a regional intelligence center fuses local intelligence with national intelligence, a local vulnerability could lead to a compromise of the sources or methods from signals intelligence, imagery intelligence, or human intelligence. A recent incident illustrates the vulnerability introduced by efforts to fuse information among different levels of government. In California, two intelligence analysts have pleaded guilty to mishandling classified material by providing it to a local law enforcement organization. Larry Richards, a detective with the Los Angeles County Sheriff's Department and a reserve colonel in the Marine Corps, allegedly recruited Gary Maziarz and Eric. L. Froboese to provide terrorism-related intelligence that they had access to in their official positions at Camp Pendleton. Richards requested information about terrorist or suspected terrorist cases in Southern California—some classified Top Secret—which Maziarz and Froboese retrieved and transmitted. Maziarz testified that he felt he was helping overcome the obstacles that prevent information-sharing among military and civilian government agencies.[16]

If this incident is indicative of prevailing pressures to share information, it sets up the participants to be vulnerable to multiple types of technical or operational exploitation. Often, the urgency to share information—especially when coupled with incompatible or inconvenient communications systems—causes parties to share information outside secure channels or to fall prey to ruses, deception, or other stratagems leading to inadvertent revelation of information to adversaries.

To address the risk of loss of shared intelligence to gangs, criminal groups, terrorist groups, or foreign intelligence, the HSINT community needs to take several actions, beginning with defining the protective measures that ensure the confidentiality of the information and information-sharing systems. Security alone will not suffice, however. Well-financed or sophisticated adversaries have the means to recruit or infiltrate organizations with access to information, or engage in espionage by technological exploitation. Counterintelligence—the discipline of identifying, penetrating, and neutralizing adversaries' attempts to collect and analyze friendly intelligence—is a necessary component. If gangs, organized criminal groups, and terrorist groups are collecting information on homeland security and law enforcement operations, there are established steps that can be taken to detect and manipulate that collection. If criminal or terrorist groups (or their affiliates) have operational assets— recruited, coerced, or infiltrated insiders—there are standard proven methods to detect and turn them. Just as HSINT is an inchoate art that differs from the work the intelligence community has traditionally done, counterintelligence for homeland security will require novel approaches to counter the intelligence collection efforts of transnational groups as opposed to foreign intelligence services.

Unfortunately, the HSINT community has not explored these concepts to any depth,[17] and the difficulties of implementing counterintelligence are daunting, given that information-sharing systems have already been established and are operational. Since the HSINT community is highly diffuse, a centralized approach would leave major vulnerabilities at every fringe node of the network. A strong counterintelligence program at one fusion center may simply redirect the adversary to another region. Although the challenges in creating an effective counterintelligence program to protect HSINT are formidable, the high stakes demand that we succeed. If an adversary has insight into homeland security or law enforcement operations, he can undermine, negate, or manipulate them. If trust begins to break down within the HSINT community, the entire information-sharing apparatus may collapse. There is an urgent need for counterintelligence analysis and operations to support the HSINT community. This support may begin with awareness training, risk assessments, and implementation of strict Operations Security (OPSEC), but it must ultimately be a nationwide effort coordinated by DHS as the primary steward of HSINT. Without such a high-level effort, all HSINT collection and analysis are at risk.

CONCLUSION

After 9/11, the need for reform became clear. The counterterrorism effort had several gaps, including poor connections among federal agencies; minimal information exchange between federal government agencies and state, local, and tribal governments; and negligible information exchange between the public and private sectors. The first phase of HSINT reform was to institute a number of processes to help fill the void between domestic and foreign intelligence. The HSINT community and its infrastructure are far from complete, however. The second phase of HSINT reform must provide (1) clearer mechanisms for collection and processing, (2) better communication for risk-based decisions, and (3) stronger counterintelligence support of homeland security operations.

Government reform is easiest in the wake of a highly publicized failure of an agency or activity. Publicly visible failures make a strong case for reform because they create general agreement on the nature of the breakdown and the changes that will address them. In some cases, especially when the cause is a lack of an organization to perform a task rather than a malfunction of an existing organization, the urgency to implement reform can mask and prolong the underlying problem rather than addressing it satisfactorily. In the case of HSINT, the failure was real, and the urgency to address it was valid. The activities put into place as a result, however, have only incrementally addressed the problem due to inattention to clear definitions, roles, and responsibilities. One can argue over the value of HSINT as currently constructed, but argument on either side leads to the same basic need for reform. If current information collection and exchange do not have value, then reform is required to ensure that the nation is not wasting time, resources, and talent. If it does have value, then reform is required to ensure that the collection and exchanges are properly protected from adversaries who can also benefit from their value.

Government reform absent a failure is more difficult, requiring leadership to identify the issues and persuade others of their importance and urgency. Given the investments in HSINT and the serious repercussions of another failure, the Obama administration needs to review the situation and address the foundational issues that threaten to compromise the entire endeavor.

ENDNOTES - CHAPTER 7

1. The views expressed here belong solely to the author and do not reflect positions of the U.S. Government or CENTRA Technology, Inc.

2. U.S. Congress, "National Commission on Terrorist Attacks upon the United States," *The 9/11 Commission Report: Final Report of the National Commission on Terrorist Attacks upon the United States,* Washington, DC: U.S. Government Printing Office, 2004, p. 263.

3. House Committee on Homeland Security, "Homeland Security Intelligence: Its Relevance and Limitations," Hearing before the Subcommittee on Intelligence, Information Sharing, and Terrorism Risk Assessment of the Committee on Homeland Security, Washington, DC: 111th Cong., 1st Sess., March 18, 2009, p. 3.

4. Mark A. Randol, *Homeland Security Intelligence: Perceptions, Statutory Definitions, and Approaches*, RL 33616, Washington, DC: Congressional Research Service, January 2009.

5. Senate Select Committee on Intelligence, Intelligence Reform and Homeland Security Intelligence, Hearing before the Senate Select Committee on Intelligence, Washington, DC: 110th Cong, 1st Sess., January 25, 2007, pp. 4–5.

6. Alex Martin and Peter Wilson, "The Value of Non-Governmental Intelligence: Widening the Field," *Intelligence and National Security* Vol. 23, No. 6, December 2008, pp. 767–776.

7. Progress in Implementing 9/11 Commission Recom-mendations, Washington, DC: Department of Homeland Security, July 22, 2009, p. 11.

8. Hamilton Bean, "Exploring the Relationship between Homeland Security Information Sharing and Local Emergency Preparedness," *Homeland Security Affairs*, Vol V, No. 2, May 2009.

9. See for example, the testimony of John W. Gaissert, Douglas C. Gillespie, and Joan T. McNamara before the Subcommittee

on Intelligence, Information Sharing, and Terrorism Risk Assessment of the Committee on Homeland Security, March 18, 2009.

10. Elizabeth Jackson, William L. McGill, and Christopher Geldart, "Regional Risk Analysis: A Coordinated Effort," Washington, DC: George Mason University, April 2009.

11. Bean, p. 10.

12. Jin Kim and William M. Allard, "Intelligence Preparation of the Battlespace: A Methodology for Homeland Security Intelligence Analysis," *SAIS Review*, Vol XXVIII, No. 1, Winter-Spring 2008.

13. Associated Press, "U.S. Embassy Agent: I Spied for Mexican Cartel," October 27, 2008.

14. Tom Jackman, "Fairfax Officer Admits Misusing Computers; Plea Entered in Illegal License Checks," *Washington Post*, February 1, 2008, p. B1; Department of Justice, Press Release, "Fairfax County Police Sergeant Pleads Guilty to Unauthorized Computer Access," January 31, 2008.

15. For one discussion of the collection and use of intelligence for law enforcement, see Stephen G. Serrao, "Intelligence-Led Policing," *Law Officer*, Vol. 5, Issue 7, July 1, 2009, p. 10.

16. Rick Rogers, "Marine Took Files as Part of Spy Ring," *San Diego Union-Tribune*, October 6, 2007; Tony Perry, "Marine Reservist Pleads Guilty to Leaking Intelligence Documents," *Los Angeles Times*, June 12, 2009.

17. For one discussion of the need for counterintelligence support of infrastructure protection, see John MacGaffin, "Counterintelligence and Infrastructure Protection," *Security in the Information Age: New Challenges, New Strategies*, Washington, DC: Joint Economic Committee, May 2002.

CHAPTER 8

WINNING HEARTS AND MINDS: FROM SLOGAN TO LEADERSHIP STRATEGY

Todd L. Pittinsky

A consensus is emerging from many different corners that winning hearts and minds is necessary to achieve goals such as stamping out world terrorism, replacing dictatorships with democracies, and controlling global warming. But can we say we know how to do it?

The term "winning hearts and minds" has been in use at least since the 1950s, when the British colonial authorities in Malaya took steps to win the trust and loyalty of rural Malayans so that they would not support the army of the Malayan Communist Party. The approach itself—one variety of what Joseph Nye termed "soft power"[1]—is far older; the imperial Romans were successful not only in conquering others, but in inspiring them to want to be Romans. The United States, the Soviet Union, and China—the three most powerful countries of the last 65 years—each significantly augmented its power by winning hearts and minds, as well as by using coercion and brute force.

Yet this indispensible approach to international relations is far from being a well-established strategy. Many of the efforts carried out by private, government, and third-sector players can be seen as overly simplistic—a little like King Kong clumsily wooing Fay Wray *after* wreaking havoc on New York City. As a social scientist, I cannot help noticing that, at least in the literature and most likely in the field too, many of these efforts are poorly defined. Perhaps more troubling, they have a patchwork quality of simply trying things that seem logical, such as economic aid or variations on brand marketing, with too little guidance from theory and empirical research. Would we develop a new weapon without a solid scientific basis? Would we develop a new weapon with only a vague, metaphorical description of what it will do? Of course not. Yet we have been racing ahead with efforts to win hearts and minds without a clear definition of what winning hearts and minds actually means and without scientific inquiry into how it works.

As a result, winning hearts and minds is still more of a slogan than a comprehensive strategy. The goal of this chapter is to unravel some of the confusion over what winning hearts and minds really can do, who can do it, and when it can be done.

A FUNDAMENTAL LEADERSHIP TASK

Leadership, at its core, is typically conceived and taught as the skill of guiding a group of people — for whom one has some formal or at least acknowledged responsibility and over whom one has some formal or at least acknowledged authority — to accomplish a desired goal. Yet accomplishing the goal often requires the cooperation and even the active participation of people who are not in any sense the leader's followers and may even be opponents.[2] A military commander, for example, may be pursuing a goal which cannot be achieved without the cooperation of a local population which is indifferent, afraid, or even actively hostile. If one achieves military victory, one acquires yet another problematic constituency — one's defeated enemies. For a vivid demonstration that "leading" one's defeated enemies can be managed in better or worse ways, compare the outcomes of World War I and World War II. Somehow, German and Japanese hearts and minds were significantly won over after World War II in a way that German hearts and minds were not won over after World War I.

What all this means is that winning hearts and minds is a *fundamental* leadership task. It is not an extra task on top of the *real* tasks — delegated to the "hearts and minds department" and expendable if push comes to shove — but a natural and necessary part of such leadership mandates as making the United States safe from terrorist attacks and catalyzing international cooperation on global warming. It is certainly part of the lofty ambition of moving closer to the day when all the nations of the world work together on shared goals in a spirit of positive — rather than grudging or strategic — interdependence.

Furthermore, winning hearts and minds is a leadership task because it is inherently forward-looking. Management is often seen as dealing with the ups and downs of the status quo while leadership is seen as envisioning a future and mobilizing followers to create it. While specific short-term political, economic, or military goals often seem to call for timely and effective management, leaders always need to recognize and seize the opportunity to win hearts and minds, even when that long-term goal clashes with important short-term goals. The alternative to seizing the opportunity may not simply be losing the opportunity, but losing those same hearts and minds. The American and British leaders of the 2003 invasion of Iraq (March 20 to May 1) had specific short-term goals: "To disarm Iraq of weapons of mass destruction (WMD), to end Saddam Hussein's support for terrorism, and to free the Iraqi people."[3] Winning hearts and minds was neither explicitly nor implicitly part of the plan. But, as we all learned, ignoring hearts and minds was not truly an option. Failing to win over hearts and minds, we seriously hardened them, which in turn made the military, political, and economic objectives that much harder to achieve.

We are increasingly conscious of the importance of winning hearts and minds and we are more committed to it, but the efforts are still sporadic and unanchored. A theatrical speech by President Obama in Cairo, a bold commitment to stepped-up diplomacy by Secretary of State Clinton (even while the position of undersecretary for public diplomacy and global affairs remained empty)—are these the proper steps? What should be guiding these efforts? Where should leaders look for wisdom?

TAPPING THE UNTAPPED REALM OF ALLOPHILIA

One can think of winning hearts and minds as an area of applied social science. Like the social sciences, our current discourse on winning hearts and minds suffers from a bias—a tilt toward the negative. For historical reasons, the social sciences have focused a lot of attention over the last 50 years on the nature, causes, and reversal of generalized negative attitudes about groups (hate prejudices), ranging from the white prejudices against African Americans and the anti-Semitism in Europe which erupted in the Holocaust (the two which sparked much of this research) to a more recent interest in the prejudices which many Westerners and Arabs have about each other. Lost in the research shuffle—and the interventions that the research has sparked—was the fact that people can and do have generalized positive as well as negative feelings about members of different groups. We have invested in understanding how to get groups to hate each other less; we have sorely underinvested in understanding how to get groups to like each other more.

Winning hearts and minds, while not inherently focused on situations characterized initially by ill will, suffers from the same negative bias. Winning hearts and minds tends to get attention when the negative feelings (ranging from distaste to hatred) of another group stand in the way of one's own group achieving a goal. For example, the United States is negotiating with Colombia for access to seven Colombian military bases; this has met with resistance from other Latin American countries with historical reasons to fear U.S. bullying.

While a focus on the negative—on *undoing* bad feelings and hatred—seems perfectly sensible, it is, in fact, one of the obstacles to making winning hearts and minds more reliably effective. It is simply too one-sided, like a science of medicine that has much to say about illness but nothing to say about health.

Recent social science research into *allophilia*—positive attitudes toward a group different from one's own—may hold keys to more successful strategies for winning hearts and minds. A key finding is that allophilia is not simply the opposite of prejudice. Positive and negative feelings about a group are distinct phenomena, largely (though not entirely) independent of each other, and quite able to coexist. Think, for example, of income and debt. High debt is not the same thing as lack of income; high income is not the same thing as lack of debt. Changing one's debt does not change one's income. Changing one's income may or may not change one's debt, and it will always be best if one can increase income *and* reduce debt. In the same way, to achieve a healthy balance sheet of cross-national attitudes, our interactions with other countries must reduce prejudice but also engender allophilia.

If prejudice and allophilia are not simply the opposites of each other, it would follow—and research shows—that they have *causes* which are not simply the opposites of each other. For example, competition for employment or for majority status in a neighborhood can be a cause of prejudice between groups. But alleviating such competition, while it may reduce the prejudice, will not be a cause of allophilia between the groups. Prejudice and allophilia also have *effects* which are not simply the opposites of each other. For example, allophilia studies have found that reducing prejudice toward a particular group will reduce hostile acts against that group; obviously an important step. It will not, however, make people more actively supportive and helpful towards members of that group. Increasing allophilia, on the other hand, can have just that effect.

What all of this means for winning hearts and minds is that there is a promising leadership path which is rarely taken. It is not enough to try to counteract prejudices. One must also actively promote allophilia. Granted, that is an "extra" task, but one that can provide benefits that the reduction of hatred— even the complete reduction of prejudice—can never provide.

Research is revealing more about this path of promoting allophilia. For example, sympathy for a group—feeling unhappy in response to that group's suffering and despair—is far more helpful for reducing prejudice than for increasing allophilia. *Symhedo-*

nia for a group — feeling joy in response to that group's success and good fortune — is more helpful for increasing allophilia than for reducing prejudice.[4] Yet we continue to commit an empathy error: We work harder to evoke sympathy than to evoke symhedonia.[5] Compare how much attention is devoted in the news media and in educational programs to encouraging Whites to feel sorry for what Blacks suffered from slavery and segregation, with how little is devoted to encouraging Whites to feel joyful for Blacks who never thought they would live to see a black President.

We are also learning more about the different effects of different ways of displaying group pride. A group can increase prejudice against itself with displays of group pride that seem arrogant, such as American soldiers toppling the statue of Saddam Hussein or Palestinians rejoicing in the street after the 9/11 attacks. A group can increase allophilia towards itself with more genuine displays of pride, such as vowing to go to the moon and then pulling it off. In much the same way that individuals are attracted to others who seem confident, groups feel allophilia for other groups that seem to have healthy pride without the excesses of narcissism and arrogance.[6]

How valuable is allophilia? American allophilia for England, the "mother country," was a decisive benefit for that ally during World War II. Allophilia for America has brought an untold number of immigrants who, collectively, have made a tremendous contribution to our economic and cultural successes. Seeing how valuable an asset this feeling is suggests that we should not leave its evolution entirely to historical chance or word of mouth, but learn more about how to acquire and maintain it deliberately. What we need now is to extend our basic research on cross-national relations to the point where we can develop a reliably effective practice of winning hearts and minds by promoting cross-national allophilia, not just reducing cross-national hatred.

UNRAVELING SOME KNOTS

In the first decades of the 20th century, a handful of thinkers realized that humans could travel in space. Their physics was quite correct, but too many of the necessary technical and organizational tools had still to be invented.[7] The practice of winning hearts and minds is at a similar juncture: rich with a promise that is being acknowledged as never before, but not as sophisticated as it needs to be. I turn now to address some of the guidelines which, if followed, will allow allophilia to take its place as a reliable leadership strategy. Specifically, I offer six principles for promoting both a richer understanding and a more effective practice of winning hearts and minds.

Do Not Wait Until Hearts and Minds Have Already Been Lost.

One hallmark of good leadership is that it prepares followers for possible futures which the leader can see coming even if his or her followers cannot—or do not want to. We seem to take winning hearts and minds most seriously when conflicts erupt and we need help from a group that is not inclined to give it. But there is nothing about winning hearts and minds that is inherently remedial. In social science terms, promoting allophilia is not the same as reducing prejudice and it can—indeed should—be promoted even when there is no prejudice to reduce. Winning hearts and minds can be carried out any time and, in fact, should be carried out all the time, recognizing that conflicts will arise and that, when they do, friends will be able to work through them better than strangers or enemies. Friends are more likely than strangers or enemies to forgive each other's trespasses.

Winning hearts and minds as a consistent strategy will be much more effective, not to mention moral, than repeatedly trying to win hearts and minds to patch up a bad spell in foreign relations. Margarita Krochik and Tom Tyler point out, for the context in which a leader's followers are divided into disharmonious subgroups, that one way to lead is to reward each subgroup for its cooperation. But the researchers recognize that this is a vulnerable strategy: "Leaders cannot always deliver rewards. . . . In fact, they are especially unlikely to be able to do so during times of crisis or change, when member support is most needed." [8] Consistently treating others fairly, the authors conclude, is a more sustainable leadership strategy, a more reliable way of winning hearts and minds "for a rainy day." It is also a more sustainable strategy for winning *and keeping* hearts and minds; more opportunistic strategies for doing so are likely to break down when most needed.

The more each country's well-being depends on what the people and governments of other countries think of it—a hallmark of the modern age—the more that winning hearts and minds should be seen as a crucial form of national security and a crucial diplomatic resource, standard operating procedure in good weather and bad.

Think Beyond "Guns and Butter."

For some, winning hearts and minds begins and ends with economic aid. But as its very name implies, winning hearts and minds needs to address more than people's material needs. In the long run, the stomach — even a full stomach — is not the way to the heart. People whom America has helped materially can still have very negative attitudes toward America and Americans. America helped arm Muslims fighting the Soviet occupation of Afghanistan in the 1980s, but some of those same Muslims were as opposed to the infidel West as they were to godless Communism.[9]

Economic aid typically addresses the lowest levels of Maslow's hierarchy of needs — physical survival and safety — but not the higher levels — love and belonging, esteem, and self-actualization.[10] Let us consider just one of the many possible forms of self-actualization — the satisfaction of curiosity. Few government incentives have been developed to send people to the Web for information about and contact with other countries. On the contrary, some governments have tried mightily to stifle this form of self-actualization. Yet, in the last decade, we have seen global confirmation of this "need" in the ever-growing use of the Internet to reach out to the world. An economic or educational aid policy that ignored the popular wish to be connected to the rest of the world (or that perhaps stifled the wish in cahoots with the recipient nation's less-than-democratic government) would not be likely to win hearts and minds, however materially generous the program was.

To understand the power of needs other than material needs, think of your attachment to your own country. Most Americans would balk at the suggestion

174

that they love their country merely because different levels of government provide safety from crime, fire, starvation, polio, food poisoning, mineshaft collapse, and so on. They would point to freedom and opportunity (however loosely and variously defined), to jazz and country music, to skateboarding and baseball, to Broadway and Hollywood. Any other country or people will also have such a list.

In much the same way, our positive attachments to other nations are based on more than material needs being sated. Is the American feeling for the United Kingdom (UK) based on its exports? (How many can you even name beyond the Beatles?) Americans tend to have positive feelings about Canada, but not on account of any material benefit we get from our relationship with that country.

Count the Government In.

The phrase "winning hearts and minds" is typically associated with government actions, yet there is some understandable feeling that any government campaign to win another group's hearts and minds will be tainted from the start—mere propaganda. Even if it is not propaganda, the recipients may *assume* that it is and will not be receptive to it. For these reasons, many believe that attempts to win hearts and minds will be carried out most effectively by nongovernmental organizations (NGOs).

But are we to conclude that governments should stay out of the business of winning hearts and minds? Or rather that governments must take care to do a proper job of it? Governments undertake economic, military, medical, and other kinds of aid—sometimes accomplishing much good—despite the fact that their motives can be, and indeed often are, misconstrued.

Propaganda itself turns out to be rather hard to define. Is propaganda defined by false information or by self-serving intentions? Thousands of people come into the United States every year—legally and illegally—because they can find better-paying jobs in the United States than they can at home. But if the U.S. Government tried, for its own self-serving reasons, to convince people that they can get better-paying jobs in the United States than they can at home, would that make it propaganda? If a government has good reason to believe that it has something valuable to offer others, is it wrong to try to convince others of it? We do not object when our government tries to convince people around the world to use more productive farming techniques or to adopt practices which would prevent tapeworm. Yet many shy away from the idea of our government trying to convince people to adopt a political system that most of us believe really is better than dictatorship, oligarchy, and theocracy. Some of us are more comfortable when our government kills people in a war than when it tries to persuade them how to live.

I am not proposing here that our government should or should not try to change people's minds about how they live and how they are governed. I am proposing that we make a disciplined effort to distinguish between gut reactions and reasoned objections to government involvement in winning hearts and minds, so that we can make more rational choices about when it would or would not be good for a government to try to do so.

In any case, government will not find winning hearts and minds easy. President George W. Bush had the idea of appointing a marketing person to repair

America's image in the Middle East. During Bush's 8-year tenure, that position was held by four people whose individual and collective efforts are generally seen to have had little success. But that does not mean Bush's impulse to improve America's public diplomacy was a mistake. Many rockets fizzled (or blew up) before one made it to the moon.

While the United States has to be careful not be bombastic, it should not be unrealistically humble, either. There is too much that we should be rightly proud to share with the world. What we need is enough research and understanding to know which voices can be heard most clearly under which circumstances. In other words, we need to know what our choices are, and how to choose among them. We need practical research aimed at clarifying both the efficacy and the ethics of government efforts to win hearts and minds.

Set More Precise Goals.

Campaigns to win hearts and minds are often saddled with rather vague goals. We want "them" to "like" us, but what does that mean? It is not hard to find foreigners who wear Michael Jackson tee shirts, gulp down Coke and McDonalds' fries, and treat American visitors with great kindness, yet turn out in the streets to protest American foreign policy. Do such people "like" us or not? What do we actually need to "win" from them?

Here, the aforementioned work on allophilia provides some guideposts. Research on allophilia has identified its five specific constituents — affection, engagement, kinship, comfort, and enthusiasm.[11] These are measureable (using the Allophilia Scale),[12] enabling us to stipulate more precisely the goals that add up to winning hearts and minds. Moreover, we are enabled to evaluate which methods will accomplish one or another of those goals.

The fact that positive and negative feelings about another group are largely independent means that it is not good enough to say "they like us" or "they don't like us," or even to say, "they like/dislike us this much." A more precise science of winning hearts and minds will say (ideally): "With this much negative feeling, we can expect these particular kinds of behavior which may be obstacles to our present or future goals. At the same time, with this much of various kinds of positive feeling, we can expect these particular kinds of behavior which may be helpful in achieving our present or future goals." The helpful behavior might be joining the United States in an international treaty, or voting with the United States on a United Nations (UN) resolution, or contributing to a peacekeeping force or a military action.

Engage Two Ways.

Helena Finn, a senior American diplomat who recently served as a fellow at the Council on Foreign Relations, underscores in *Foreign Affairs* (2003) that "diplomacy is a two-way street."[13] Some efforts to win hearts and minds have fallen flat because they were not two-way enough—or at all. In 2003, the U.S. Department of State launched *Hi* magazine, aimed at winning the hearts and minds of Middle Eastern and Muslim youth. Publication was suspended after 2 1/2 years. *Hi* did not seem to have achieved any popularity with its intended audience, partly because it presented a superficially "light"[14] view of American life, while ignoring the contentious political issues that cause Arabs to have negative attitudes about America. A hearts and minds campaign called "Shared Values" seems to have made the same mistake. As an Indonesian economics student put it after watching one of the "Shared Values" TV ads: "We know that there's religious freedom in America, and we like that. What we're angry about is the arrogant behavior of the U.S. in the rest of the world."[15] In both cases, the engagement was not two-way (and therefore, not really engagement at all). The message seemed to be: We'll tell you what you should know about us and never mind about anything else.

In contrast, a Pakistani broadcaster, Aqeel Malik, launched a radio station in the Swat region specifically to win the local people's hearts and minds away from the Taliban, which had its own popular station, and toward the Pakistani military, which was trying to drive the Taliban out. Despite violent threats from the Taliban, Malik invited Taliban members to take part in phone-in discussions on the air. He wanted his audience to hear the two opposing views in full so that they would conclude for themselves that the Pakistani state would be better for them than the Taliban.[16] While we will not know for years whether his approach worked, it clearly engaged the "other" and did not seem to arouse the cynicism and suspicion that *Hi* did.

Invest in Building the Science.

The phrase "winning hearts and minds" is only a metaphor and rather hard to pin down. We use it because it has currency in the field, clearly refers to something important, and is inspiring, but we would benefit from a more precise formulation. While a military force might adopt an evocative mission statement such as "pushing the enemy into the sea," you can be sure the good commanders would have a more precise set of goals and strategies, too.

Ideas, intuitions, and suspicions about what wins hearts and minds must be subject to empirical validation. What we learn may surprise us. During the invasion of Iraq, for example, we often heard from foreign pundits around the globe that people in their country like Americans, it's America—that is, the actions of the American government or of American businesses—they strongly dislike. This is neat rhetoric but scientifically dubious; it is not clear that the human brain maintains such rigid categories as *government* and *people*. There is some experimental evidence, for example, that negative feelings about a leader (a nation's president, for example) will engender negative feelings about the leader's followers (the rest of us).[17]

A more complete commitment to winning hearts and minds must therefore support practical research on the basic processes and pathways by which it occurs. Such research must certainly be interdisciplinary. Currently international relations discourse is dominated by economists and political scientists, who too often defer to the traditional economic axiom that human beings are rational actors, despite the growing importance of nonrational actor theories. In a similar vein, a self-interest model looms over the study and practice of negotiation. A whole generation of policy students has been taught normative models of negotiation in which one should take into account the well-being of the "other," but strictly as a way of advancing one's own interests. But such models cannot explain how Tibetans, for example, have won American hearts and minds to the extent they have. Americans have no rational self-interest in Tibetan independence and much rational self-interest in good relations with China. Clearly, winning hearts and minds is not simply a matter of exploiting joint gains for self-gain.

A multidisciplinary approach is also needed to balance efficacy with appropriateness. While some disciplines may be better equipped to help us learn what will work and to understand why it does, other disciplines will be better equipped to wrestle through the thorny questions of what should and should *not* be done, irrespective of its efficacy.

GETTING STARTED: A FOUR-POINT ACTION PLAN FOR WINNING HEARTS AND MINDS

I asked in the opening paragraph: "Can we say we know how to do it?" Although we need much more research and a much greater commitment to act on the knowledge we already have, we do know enough to get started. Here are four ways the United States can win hearts and minds by steadily building and maintaining allophilia.

Citizen Diplomacy Through Social Networking Media.

It is time for citizen-to-citizen diplomacy to take advantage of the technological fact that ordinary Americans can be directly connected to people in other countries through social networking media. When the New York Philharmonic performed in North Korea, it was only 100 or so musicians performing for a very select audience. Even if broadcast to a wider North Korean audience, the concert was literally and figuratively a staged event and perhaps a bit too formal to effectively win hearts and minds. Whatever positive effect it had could be achieved many times over by letting anyone in the world with an Internet connection sit in on local American concerts, sports events, city council meetings, school plays, and so on. Imagine taking a group of ordinary Saudis, or Russians, or Colombians on an interactive visit to the local pizza parlor where they could chat with the staff and customers and maybe order up some pizzas to be delivered to a local senior center.[18] This is already possible, so the time to do it is now.

Global Citizen-Science.

The three main U.S. agencies concerned with winning hearts and minds—the Department of State, the Department of Defense, and the United States Agency for International Development (USAID)—along with other agencies, such as the Department of Education and the National Science Foundation, could promote allophilia for the United States by launching a global citizen-science network which allowed ordinary people around the world to participate in scientific research that would benefit mankind in general.[19] Medical and environmental research would be obvious examples. Such a network might be particularly effective in generating allophilia by showing the United States in the role of "servant leadership"—that is, providing moral leadership to others by being of service to them. The tools would not have to be elaborate; the longest-running citizen-science project currently active is probably the Audubon Society's very low-tech Christmas bird count. While the bird count operates only in the Americas, World Water Monitoring Day operates "from Indonesia to Arkansas" and involves only "a simple test kit" which even children can use.[20]

Virtual Visitor Centers.

Not every foreigner has a chance to get on a plane to visit the United States—nor, perhaps, should they be emitting the carbons that a flight would produce. But the United States can certainly create movable green (solar-powered) visitor centers, roughly the size of a movable house, that would travel around in other countries—public kiosks of a sort. Inside, visitors would be automatically linked to boxes in the United States so that the traveling visitor center in, say, Bolivia would become a virtual visitor center in Times Square, on the Mall in Washington, on a main street in Omaha, or on the beach in Hawaii. Webcams would show the local scene, and there would be interactive access to all sorts of other views and information.

Teaching English Online.

You can learn a lot about another culture using materials available in your own language, but cannot fully know that culture without knowing its own language. We would like people to know our culture and value its best aspects as highly as we do. People all over the world want to learn English anyway. So why not build allophilia by helping them do it? It is amazing that, in 2009, there is no U.S. Government-sponsored Web destination which people anywhere in the world can visit to learn American English (and American history and culture) through contact with the full diversity of American citizens.

All four of these suggestions can be put into action all over the world all the time (unless banned by another government). In this way, they address the need to build and maintain allophilia as a regular vital function of foreign policy rather than as a response to a crisis. These techniques and others like them could be the international relations equivalent of the healthy diet and exercise which reduce the likelihood of an ambulance ride to the emergency room.

CONCLUSION

Winning hearts and minds is a worthy, inspiring, and indeed critical goal. We are at a turning point, having learned a good deal about what makes people think well of others rather than ill. We thus can feel confident that knowing a lot more would equip our leaders with much better ways to reach for that goal.

ENDNOTES - CHAPTER 8

1. Joseph Nye, *The Powers to Lead*, New York: Oxford University Press, 2008; Joseph Nye, *Bound to Lead: The Changing Nature of American Power,* New York: Basic Books, 1990.

2. Todd L. Pittinsky. "Intergroup Leadership: What it Is, Why it Matters, and How it Is Done," in Todd Pittinsky, ed., *Crossing the Divide: Intergroup Leadership in a World of Difference*, Boston, MA: Harvard Business School Publishing Corporation, 2009.

3. Office of the White House, "President Discusses Beginning of Operation Iraqi Freedom" President's Radio, Address of the Press Secretary, March 22, 2003.

4. Todd L. Pittinsky and R. M. Montoya, "Symhedonia in Intergroup Relations: The Relationship of Empathic Joy to Prejudice and Allophilia," *Psicologia Sociale*, forthcoming.

5. Todd L. Pittinsky, *Why Hate Wins*, Cambridge, MA: Harvard Business Press, manuscript in preparation.

6. J. J. Ratcliff, Todd L. Pittinsky, and S. Simon, "The Contrasting Influence of Perceived Hubristic—And Authentic—Pride on Intergroup Relations," Poster session presented at the 10th annual meeting of the Society for Personality and Social Psychology, Tampa, FL, February 2009.

7. Frank Winter, *Prelude to the Space Age: The Rocket Societies, 1924-1940*, Washington, DC: Smithsonian Institution Press, 1983.

8. Margarita Krochik and Tom R. Tyler, "United Pluralism: Balancing Subgroup Identification and Superordinate Group Cooperation," in Todd L. Pittinsky, ed., *Crossing the Divide: Intergroup Leadership in a World of Difference*.

9. Wikipedia, "Islamic mujahid movement," available from *en.wikipedia.org/wiki/Islamic_mujahid_movement*.

10. Abraham Maslow, "A Theory of Human Motivation," *Psychological Review*, Vol. 50, No. 4, 1943, pp. 370–396.

11. Todd L. Pittinsky, S. A. Rosenthal, and R. M. Montoya, "Measuring Positive Attitudes Toward Outgroups: Development and Validation of the Allophilia Scale," in L. Tropp and R. Mallett, eds., *Beyond Prejudice Reduction: Pathways to Positive Intergroup Relations*, Washington, DC: American Psychological Association, 2009.

12. Todd L. Pittinsky, "A Two-Dimensional Theory of Intergroup Leadership: The Case of National Diversity," *American Psychologist*, forthcoming.

13. H. K. Finn, "The Case for Cultural Diplomacy: Engaging Foreign Audiences," *Foreign Affairs*, November/December 2003.

14. A. Soble, "The Business Brand of America," *The Yale Globalist*, 2009, available from *tyglobalist.org/index.php/20090404186/Focus/The-Business-of-Brand-America.html*.

15. P. L. Plaisance, "The Propaganda War on Terrorism: An Analysis of the United States' 'Shared Values' Public Diplomacy Campaign After September 11, 2001," *Journal of Mass Media Ethics*, Vol. 20, No. 4, 2005, pp. 250-268.

16. P. Reeves (Reporter), "Pakistan's Military Wins Swat Valley Radio War" [Radio series episode], E. McDonnell (Executive Producer), *Morning Edition*, Washington, DC: National Public Radio, August 31, 2009.

17. Todd L. Pittinsky, R. M. Montoya, L. R. Tropp, and A. Chen, "How and When Leader Behavior Affects Intergroup Liking: Affect, Approval, and Allophilia," in B. Mannix, M. Neale, and C. Anderson, eds., *Research on Managing Groups and Teams: Affect & Groups*, Oxford, UK: Elsevier Science Press, 2007, pp. 125–144.

18. Pittinsky, *Why Hate Wins*.

19. *Ibid.*

20. Wikipedia, "World Water Monitoring Day," available from *en.wikipedia.org/wiki/World_Water_Monitoring_Day*.

CHAPTER 9

CHANGE IS HARD . . . BUT EVEN SMALL STEPS MATTER

Jeffrey A. Engel

The history of the short generation between 1989 and 2001 matters in contemporary debates over reforming America's national security system. It matters as well to the present collection of articles, developed in 2009 while a new presidential administration was making its initial mark on the international system. This history matters because the national security bureaucracies and structures first developed to wage and win the Cold War not only survived the Cold War's demise, but more importantly largely retain their salience and structure even as the ensuing Global War on Terror approaches its 10th year. Any current or future effort to reform such a massive and long-lived system therefore confronts entrenched interests and almost unfathomable bureaucratic inertia. Meaningful reform will surely be difficult given the weight of this history. It might well be impossible.

Few would have predicted a generation ago the place America's national security system would currently occupy. Remarkable change occurred in 1989. The Cold War, that bipolar world system that had largely governed international relations since the close of World War II, began to crumble. The Berlin Wall fell. Protestors roiled China's Tiananmen Square, and more successfully fomented wholesale change through Eastern Europe. Within 2 years, even the Soviet Union would be no more.

These were golden days for American policymakers. Their Cold War "victory"—and they did perceive it as a victory— seemingly validated all that Americans had long held to be true. Never mind that, as is more common in Europe, the Cold War's end was seen simply as a communist capitulation prompted by exhaustion. For triumphalists, freedom was a universally beloved value; the unfettered market could out-produce state-run economies; and the future world, filled with democracies, would find conflict rare but American power in abundance. Because past success was seen as indicative of future returns, the future for Washington and for the world it intended to lead looked bright indeed.

We now know that such optimism was short-sighted. History did not end after communism's collapse. The 1990s were filled with small and brutal conflicts. Some, such as in Yugoslavia and Somalia, ultimately demanded American engagement, despite great reluctance within American policymaking circles to enter into military operations with no clear allies or markers of victory save the reestablishment of order. Some like Iraq demanded ongoing American vigilance and eventually large-scale military engagement. Other simmering regions of unrest, most notably Afghanistan, proved impervious to the powers of democratization and the market—the very foundations of Western progress long preached by American strategists. Afghanistan in time became not only a chaotic safe-haven for those content to live beyond the American sphere of influence, but also the launching point for attacks against the very heart of American power. The terrifying tragedy of September 11, 2001 (9/11), was not only the tragic result of chaos run amuck, but the final deathblow to post-Cold War optimism.

America's national security structure and posture

have already changed since 2001. Most notably, the omnibus reforms developed in the immediate heat of the 9/11 attacks produced from scratch a Department of Homeland Security and expanded federal powers designed to thwart and destroy international agents of terror. As any reader of this collection well knows, expansion of such powers has not been without controversy. After-shocks of this initial spasm of national security reform spawned a Director of National Intelligence some years later, and then by 2007, implementation of many of the primary recommendations offered by the 9/11 Commission. Within its first months in office, the new Obama administration even joined together the National Security and Homeland Security Councils under the seemingly more integrated umbrella of a new National Security staff.

The continuities present in today's national security structure, reaching back into the first decades of the Cold War, far exceed in salience any post-9/11 changes. The Department of Defense (DoD) remains the largest security and military organization in the world. The Central Intelligence Agency (CIA), despite its public relations difficulties following 9/11 and the Iraq War, remains the most public face for the American intelligence community (IC). The Department of Energy (DoE) has emerged as a prominent agency for investigating and thwarting potential nuclear threats, just as the Federal Bureau of Investigation (FBI) stalwartly maintains its role as the primary counter to terrorism on American soil.

More important than the mere continued existence of this alphabet soup of national security agencies is the fact that each has expanded its ranks and its budget since 2001. The CIA, for example, embarked on a well-publicized hiring expansion designed to bolster its ranks by greater than 50 percent. By the close of the George W. Bush administration, more than 100,000 federal employees worked for one of the 16 entities overseen by the Directorate of National Intelligence. Their aggregate annual budget, based on publicly announced figures, exceeded $50 billion. Estimates suggest that a similar number work as private contractors for the intelligence agencies. These are hardly inconsequential figures.

America's national security bureaucracy has expanded, both in size and scope, since 2001, and, more to the point, it has expanded largely based upon components that existed in 1989. As James Locher notes in Chapter 2 of this volume, "the U.S. national security system is arguably the largest organizational decisionmaking system in the world."[1] It is, however, still designed mainly "to overcome post-World War II threats."[2]

Reforming such a gargantuan system will surely be no easy task. Bureaucracies rarely change gracefully. Moreover, as several of our authors note, in a Washington where money so easily equates with power, political infighters not only take their own agency's agenda to heart, but come to consider the battle for resources a zero-sum game. If any meaningful effort at reform attempts to improve the national security field by piecemeal or targeted cuts, the resulting pressures will surely only exacerbate what Locher terms "interagency fratricide."[3]

Organizational theory suggests that bureaucracies typically perceive such reforms as outside impositions. They resist such change almost by nature. As Richard Immerman notes in Chapter 4 of this anthology, "Change is particularly hard, especially if [the] organization is large and its culture entrenched."[4] It would be difficult to find organizations that better fit the words "large" and "entrenched" than those that comprise America's national security apparatus. As already noted, many of its most powerful entities date to the 1940s. That is institutional memory aplenty to resist and ultimately thwart change.

The consensus of authors in this anthology is not therefore in favor of wholesale change, which might well be beyond current capabilities or desires. Taken as a whole, these contributors (excepting Locher) instead suggest smaller — though clearly important — pathways for improving the tenor, efficiency, interagency cooperation, and leadership within the intelligence field. The following pages of this chapter highlight several of the collection's key findings, best understood as suggestions on the margins of national security reform — margins, that is, as distinct from wholesale or whole of government reform. While laudable and, according to such recent findings as those by Locher's Project on National Security Reform, quite necessary, wholesale change appears beyond present capabilities and political realities. This is especially true given a President bent on domestic rather than national security reform, a Democratic Party long considered weaker on security issues than its main rival, and the lingering international threats still at hand, including the omnipresent potential for further terrorist attacks at home and abroad.

Washington's principal national security organizations survived the end of the very Cold War they were designed to win. They expanded after 9/11. They are unlikely to be reduced while a war on terror (or long war, or period of persistent conflict, or whatever term one prefers) continues. No matter the name, no end is currently in sight for that conflict. Changes at the margins of the American national security system, better described as improvements, are therefore all that is reasonably possible in the political environment for as far as the eye can currently see. Such improvements can and must matter, as the chapters in this book uniformly suggest.

This is not to deny that recipes for wholesale change exist. One will be handily offered to any political leader wise enough or foolish enough—but either way, brave enough—to accept the supremely high risks, even with their potentially high rewards.

Yes, reform is hard, and particularly so, given the emotions and dangers at play whenever national security is at stake. Contributors to this anthology agree on this point, but almost universally note that a significant roadblock to reform is the existence of numerous semi-autonomous agencies and organizations, the overarching umbrella of national security. The very fact that different agencies exist, with mandates that intentionally overlap, leads inevitably to interagency competition and tension.

Some argue that such tension is productive, improving efficiency while ensuring, as the nation's founders would have desired, that no single political entity garners too much power at the expense of others or, more fundamentally, of liberty. In a passage noted in Immerman's chapter from Amy Zegart, such bureaucratic infighting has a long pedigree. He writes, "The pathologies that afflicted the [Intelligence Community], . . . inherent organizational defects, bureaucratic self-interest, and fragmentation most prominently, were unaffected by the Cold War's termination."[5]

Recognizing the impossibility of eliminating interagency tension wholesale, several authors within this volume offer suggestions for limiting it in order to improve the system's overall efficiency. Geoffrey French (Chapter 7), for example, suggests ways to improve information sharing and simultaneously enhance counterintelligence capabilities across the spectrum of current agencies. "There is an urgent need for counterintelligence analysis and operations to support the [Homeland Security Intelligence] community," he writes. "This may begin with awareness training, risk assessments, and support to Operations Security (OPSEC), but it must ultimately be a nation-wide effort coordinated by DHS as the primary steward of HSINT."[6]

Immerman similarly notes the power of reforming the IC through development (and ultimately, the imposition) of shared values, language, and standards. He participated in one such reform effort. The experience left him, by his own admission, truly surprised by its possibilities. "I argued at that time [before joining the IC] and subsequently that the problems that afflicted the U.S. intelligence community were so pervasive, and reflected such an array of dynamics — political, psychological, and cultural — that they were all but impervious to institutional reforms."[7]

Immerman now thinks differently, offering an example of how reform can be realized by dedicated individuals devoted to a common goal. Analysts and employees from disparate agencies will better integrate their work and thus meet their shared goals if jointly trained in a shared language. "The culture of distinctiveness (which is often almost mythic) and competition among the elements remains pervasive, and often defiant," he writes. "The consequences are extremely detrimental for information sharing, especially when juxtaposed with a reflexive disposition toward secretiveness and the widespread belief that secrets are the key ingredients of power."[8] Change can overcome such obstacles, he notes, only incrementally. But it can come. "Even if not perfect," he concludes of the reform movement he participated in, "there is greater collaboration and integration throughout the IC."[9] Such reforms can be a model for others.

Other authors within this collection reach similar conclusions. James Goldgeier, for example, a scholar particularly versed in the evolution of American national security strategy since 1989, suggests several potential improvements of his own in Chapter 5. These include reinforcing the current administration's emphasis on economic issues (several notches above the level reached by its predecessors), but also improving the overall economic sophistication of security policymakers whose principal areas of responsibility did not in the past typically touch the economic sphere. "The community of foreign policy experts tends not to have a lot of economic expertise," he writes. "This became a huge problem in the Clinton efforts to bridge the gap. When a principal such as Robert Rubin or Lawrence Summers explained a policy prescription by emphasizing the nature of international markets, it was hard for those on the national security side to counter those arguments; the national security types didn't have the economic knowledge (or reputation) to counter."[10]

Economic concerns are quite unlikely to diminish in importance in the future, given current financial uncertainty and the ever-quickening pace of globalization. Thus Goldgeier suggests expanding the Obama administration's recent economics push across the span of the national security field. At the same time, he wisely notes, "We should not just think of this as a one-way street. It would also be useful if those in the

NEC and Treasury Department had a strong enough grounding in national security issues not to believe that all questions can be reduced to the issue of how markets are likely to respond."[11]

Whereas Immerman, French, and Goldgeier suggest an improved common vocabulary as a means of reforming national security—be that language one of intelligence standards or economics—James Locher seeks improvement through an alteration of the bureaucracy's very structure. His suggestions for reform are the most far-reaching found within this collection. Still, they are best considered as reforms of the current system rather than institution of something wholly different. Chief among his suggestions is creation of "A cadre of National Security Executives (NSEs) appointed by the president [who] would have formal authority over interagency teams. The NSEs should be highly respected individuals who are experts in their specialty areas and known for their leadership abilities. A National Security Professional Corps should be created to recruit and retain qualified personnel."[12]

Locher contends that this new cadre of NSEs would help streamline the flow of information and thus enhance the effectiveness of national security organizations. Even more to the point, they would be able to do much the same for the interagency process as well. In the final analysis, such a program holds the promise of a better system, though not altogether a new and different one. Locher makes a point of achieving progress by improving on current practice. "The existing National Security Education Consortium (established by Executive Order 13434) should serve as the foundation for developing a comprehensive professional education and training program. This program will focus on nurturing skills and a positive culture throughout the system."[13]

It should be noted that Locher, and the Project on National Security Reform he represents, aspires to more fundamental changes than those treated above. "The 9/11 Commission report noted," he wrote, that "'Americans should not settle for incremental, ad hoc adjustments to a system designed generations ago for a world that no longer exists.' We at PNSR definitely agree!"[14] It is emblematic of the size of the problems facing any proponent of fundamental reform, and indicative of the experience-based wisdom that Locher brings to this debate (including major reform efforts in the U.S. military's special operations and joint organizations, as well as in Bosnia's defense ministry), that his call for wholesale reform is best understood not as an overhaul of the system but rather as a tune-up.

Alongside suggestions for reforming the system's structure are suggestions for improving its intent as well. Joel Rosenthal (Chapter 3) has such a suggestion, designed to enhance the ethical training and thus consciousness of national security policymakers and those they oversee, in order to produce not only a more efficient system, but a fairer and wiser one as well. He notes in particular that ethical training can produce otherwise overlooked solutions to seemingly insoluable problems. "Ethics expands the range of choices we have in front of us," he writes. "It is about creating new possibilities."[15]

Rosenthal's suggestion should not be dismissed lightly, given the divisive debates over American national security policy since 2001, which question not only the aims of such policy but more fundamentally the justifications policymakers have employed on behalf of certain decisions made under the banner of preserving security. The ongoing debate over torture and indefinite internment are good examples. Lawyers, doctors, accountants, and even university professors routinely undertake ethical training throughout the length of their careers. Should we demand no less of those in the national security community (not just within the military) charged with preserving our security, and, even more profoundly, with maintaining and deploying the vast arsenal of power the United States today wields in defense of its interests at home and overseas?

Rosenthal is no doubt correct in his claim that any meaningful reform of the nation's national security institutions must include further attention to ethics. Accepting his contention that ethical training illuminates heretofore unseen options, and coupling that with the general thrust of this collection that whole of government change is perhaps beyond present capabilities, Rosenthal's most valuable contribution may well be his contention that ethics can help point an individual or an organization in the correct direction. Indeed, the best heading might merely be a slight adjustment or tweak to the current course, if only we possessed the proper knowledge of our ultimate destination, informed by more discriminating ethical consideration.

Our contributors, much like the majority of those who write in the field of ethics, are concerned with improving the effectiveness and efficiency of the current national security system. They speak in terms of interagency cooperation and streamlining process. Broad-based ethical training can help diminish the drag of bureaucratic inertia, including preoccupation with institutional self-interest and a tendency to confine thinking within mental silos. Ethical training achieves such improvements by helping organizational members better appreciate the real meaning of their duties and jobs in terms of the old-fashioned but noble ideals of providing public service and promoting national interests. The ultimate goal of all CIA, FBI, and DoD employees is not, in the final analysis, to increase their organization's status, power, or abilities. It is not even to help their organization meet their stated missions. It is, instead, to improve the lives of Americans; to protect and enhance their security; and by extension to improve peace and security throughout the world. Further ethical training might well help national security operatives and workers keep that goal at the forefront of their thinking whenever a request for information or assistance arrives from another (competing) agency. With their shared national goals in mind, operational streamlining, information sharing, and, yes, reform might well occur without the need for radical systemic change.

At the least, such training in ethics might well inform American image-enhancing initiatives, such as offered by Todd Pittinsky in his provocative essay in Chapter 8, aimed at improving American security by improving the country's standing and regard throughout the world. "Winning the hearts and minds" of an adversary and, of equal import, of allies and neutrals throughout the world, is a national aim with a long and, as Pittinsky well notes, dubious pedigree. It was a fundamental maxim of American policy in the Vietnam War, for example. That war casts a long shadow over any contemporary use of the slogan. Yet the goal remains no less valid today than in the 1960s. It remains as much a slogan as a workable platform, however. To make it a credible and realizable goal, Pittinsky offers four suggestions designed to spark debate on imaginative, research-based programs for fundamentally improving America's standing in the world. As he argues, recent such efforts have been marked by "a patchwork quality of simply 'trying things' that seem logical, such as economic aid or variations on brand marketing, with too little guidance from theory and empirical research."[16] Bringing more social science and empirical thinking into the mix might well produce better results, or at the least results more in line with stated goals. This is yet another example of change and reform that can alter the system's effectiveness without a top-to-bottom overhaul.

Some suggestions for reform, while holding potential, would be hard to implement and, no doubt, harder for Congress to regulate. Among these are Andrew Preston's keen observations (Chapter 6) on the importance of thoughtful solidarity among occupants of an administration's key posts, particularly the position of national security adviser, typically the gatekeeper for issues presented to the President. "The National Security Adviser possesses an extraordinary and unrivalled authority over both policy and process in the making and implementing of U.S. foreign policy," he writes. "Ideally the National Security Adviser should be an 'honest broker,' and it is no coincidence that this term is usually used to describe the Adviser's ideal performance."[17] Preston, an authority on the first truly "modern" national security adviser, McGeorge Bundy, who served under John Kennedy and Lyndon Johnson, notes that successive occupants have tried to duplicate Bundy's political acumen, intelligence, and knowledge not only of the security field, but of the President himself. Bundy was expert in both. He well knew that the National Security Adviser, appointed without senate confirmation, had a constituency of one. He knew Kennedy well, and considered his role to be confined to serving the President alone. He never reached as complete a relationship with Lyndon Johnson, and arguably his effort to win Johnson's trust—something he enjoyed in spades with Kennedy—led him to advise what he believed the new President desired to hear, rather than what he should hear.

Of all those who have tried their hand at this sensitive yet crucial post, Preston notes, Brent Scowcroft is generally regarded as the most successful:

> Historians of the NSC are virtually unanimous in their praise of Brent Scowcroft's tenure as National Security Adviser. It helped that Scowcroft was personally close to Bush; when Scowcroft spoke, few doubted that he also spoke for the President. It also helped that Scowcroft knew the NSC system intimately—after all, he had already been National Security Adviser, under President Gerald Ford, and he had served on the Tower Commission. Scowcroft also established a good working relationship with Secretary of State James A. Baker and Secretary of Defense Dick Cheney. Scowcroft was generally fair in acting as the President's gatekeeper on foreign policy, yet he also possessed strong views of his own and at times, such as during Operations DESERT SHIELD and DESERT STORM in the Persian Gulf, acted as an especially committed policy advocate. Most important, Scowcroft smoothed relations among departments and agencies by instituting several interagency working groups that would keep lines of communication open and forestall bureaucratic turf wars that resulted from the hoarding of information. Chief among these were the Principals Committee, which Scowcroft himself chaired, and the Deputies Committee, which his own deputy, Robert Gates, chaired. Overall, though his system did not always function smoothly, Scowcroft acted as an effective manager and advocate by integrating his own views within a larger, more coordinated network.[18]

Moreover, Preston praises the significant role Scowcroft played as the administration's "honest broker."[19] Despite having strong opinions of their own, ideal national security advisers, according to Preston, manage the security team without prejudice, even while acting as players in their own right. For the national security system to function best, he concludes, it must have not just a beating heart—a President interested in keeping the system functioning—but a proper pacemaker as well, a role played by the National Security Adviser.

How to ensure that the right person rises to the position is, of course, problematic. The President alone selects this most intimate of advisers. One can only hope that current and future occupants of this important position are versed in economics as well as security (as Goldgeier would require); trained in the language and standards of intelligence (Immerman and French); capable as a manager of highly motivated people and effective, integrated organizations (Locher); but also trained in ethics in order to put all this knowledge to the proper use (Rosenthal). Oh, yes, it is best if he or she is also a personal intimate of the President, but possessed of remarkably little ego (Preston).

In the final analysis, Preston's hard-to-match criteria matter all the more, given the overall thrust of this collection that fundamental change lies beyond the ken of the presently possible. This is so because the keystone position of national security adviser is, as is so much of our security structure, the product of an earlier era. Would we create the position anew if it did not already exist? Probably. But can we hope to instill in an existing position the authority to synthesize, organize, and ultimately manage the President's entire national security agenda, given the precedents now established as fact? That is a far less likely prospect. "The National Security Adviser is . . . a Cold War innovation," Preston argues, "that has proven adept at confronting the globalized challenges of the post-Cold War world."[20] It is a position that has always been in flux, and thus more open to change than most within Washington. It might well be the position from which real change can in the future spring, so long as the President chooses its occupant wisely. One is reminded, however, when considering its potential role as catalyst for change, of the famous dictum offered as an epigraph to Dean Acheson's magisterial memoir. "If I had been present at the creation," King Alphonso X of Spain declared, "I would have given some useful hints for the better ordering of the universe."[21] It is crucial to note Alphonso's implicit recognition that a world already in existence cannot be altered as easily as one still being formed. We inherit a world, a national security bureaucracy, and, yes, even a national security adviser. It is too late to form an optimal system based on hindsight. Rather, all that remains is to move forward at the best speed possible.

For all their myriad suggestions, intermingled disciplinary approaches, and rich experience, the contributors to this collection arrive at a common fundamental point: while surely difficult, change is indeed necessary. It is best and most likely accomplished in the current political environment at the margins of the system, by making the current national security system (itself still hostage to its Cold War origins) more efficient, more responsive to interagency needs and requirements, more ethical, more mindful of the economic dimension of international relations, and more in line with desired outcomes. Such reforms are better classified as fine-tuning improvements rather than seismic shifts. But small improvements are not to be minimized. They are needed for a truly efficient system of national security to emerge. As the old maxim suggests, every journey, no matter how long, begins with a single step. The suggestions offered in the preceding chapters would make for significant first steps indeed.

But what if we truly wanted to overhaul the system, to change its fundamentals, not simply improve it at the margins? Then yet a different maxim might be in order. George Marshall, chief strategist of the American military effort in World War II and later Secretary of State, was fond throughout his career of a wise saying attributed to many before and since: the first rule of holes is, when in one, stop digging.

Marshall's maxim suggests two potential means of achieving true reform of the national security system during the first term of this new administration and after. First, stop digging. The Cold War system that remains largely in place even today needs no new elements. It needs no new bureaucracies, nor more levels within the bureaucracies. To date, the U.S. Government spends more on defense than the rest of the world combined spends on its defense. Its national security apparatus dwarfs any similar national structure throughout the world. Given the amorphous nature of Washington's adversaries in the War on Terror in particular, current American resources devoted to halting terrorism and other transnational agents of anarchy are surely disproportional to the mischief that potential terrorist organizations can inflict. More than 200,000 federal employees and private contractors contribute to the American intelligence community. Far more than that, in and out of uniform, work for the defense community. Al Qaeda's supporters might exceed these numbers. Surely, however, even the most frightening estimate of the organization's actual ranks does not.

We do not need to mobilize more counters to such threats. On the contrary, our authors suggest that the current system needs streamlining, more information sharing, better interagency integration, and a better means of defeating Washington's real national security foe: its own bureaucratic inertia. Neither new agencies, new security czars, nor new funded mandates will necessarily make the system more responsive or more capable of meeting post-Cold War transnational threats. "More" will in all likelihood not make America safer, but instead will only make the hole we find ourselves in deeper still.

How then to begin climbing out of the hole we presently occupy? One simple solution would be to make our current security agencies do more with less. Given that their parochial interests will, by the very nature of organizations and bureaucracies, inspire them to fight the least nano-cut to their resources, payrolls, and missions, a viable solution might be across-the-board cuts. If the entire national security apparatus was slashed by 20 percent across the board, each agency would be forced to do with less. But if forced to do the same job with fewer resources, they would of necessity be forced to cooperate, to share across agencies, to eliminate mission overlap and redundancy, to improve their efficiency. Because we know the trained and dedicated men and women charged with defending and enhancing American security will not consider failure an option, they will find a way to do with less. Such a suggestion for reform and improvement would be enhanced by incentives—not so much the positive incentive of the carrot, but the negative incentive of the stick. The stick, in the form of diminished budgets and resources, would bring change by necessity, if not by virtue.

This model of enhancing efficiency and improving effectiveness through resource starvation without a precipitous decline in performance is harsh, but also market tested. Many American businesses in the 1990s and after, through times of recession and prosperity alike, employed new technologies and new methods of information sharing to cut payrolls without hindering outputs. Efficiency was the mantra of the era for business. Why do we expect less of government employees and the legions of contractors who presently complement their work, than we would of profit-seeking firms? Are national security operatives, analysts, and agents less inclined to succeed than their fellow citizens in the private sector? If true change is desired, the first rule of holes is to stop digging. But the second rule is that everyone in the hole should work together to get out. Rather than demanding new shovels, rather than suggesting new plans for constructing a ladder, rather even than digging in different places, the current national security legions should simply stop digging, and start getting out. That would be real reform.

ENDNOTES - CHAPTER 9

1. James R. Locher, Chapter 2, "Leadership, National Security, and the Whole of Government Reforms: The Project on National Security Reform (PNSR) Perspective," in Joseph R. Cerami and Jeffrey A. Engel, eds., *Rethinking Leadership and "Whole of Government" National Security Reform: Problems, Progress, and Prospects*, Carlisle, PA, Strategic Studies Institute, 2010, pp. 29-47, p. 34.

2. *Ibid.*, p. 30.

3. *Ibid.*, p. 33.

4. Richard Immerman, Chapter 4, "Transforming Intelligence Analysis: 'The Tail that Wags the Dog'," in Joseph R. Cerami and Jeffrey A. Engel, eds., *Rethinking Leadership and "Whole of Government" National Security Reform: Problems, Progress, and Prospects*, Carlisle, PA, Strategic Studies Institute, 2010, pp. 73-110, p. 73.

5. *Ibid.*, p. 77.

6. Geoffrey French, Chapter 7, "Leading the Next Phase of Homeland Security Intelligence: Providing Better Definitions, Roles, and Protections," in Joseph R. Cerami and Jeffrey A. Engel, eds., *Rethinking Leadership and "Whole of Government" National Security Reform: Problems, Progress, and Prospects*, Carlisle, PA, Strategic Studies Institute, 2010, p. 149-163, p. 161.

7. Immerman, p. 75.

8. *Ibid.*, p. 101.

9. *Ibid.*, p. 103.

10. James Goldgeier, Chapter 5, "Reforming the National Security Process in a Globalizing World," in Joseph R. Cerami and Jeffrey A. Engel, eds., *Rethinking Leadership and "Whole of Government" National Security Reform: Problems, Progress, and Prospects*, Carlisle, PA, Strategic Studies Institute, 2010, p. 111-125, p. 123.

11. *Ibid.*, p. 124.

12. Locher, p. 44.

13. *Ibid.*, p. 45.

14. *Ibid.*, p. 45.

15. Joel H. Rosenthal, Chapter 3, "Leadership as Practical Ethics," in Joseph R. Cerami and Jeffrey A. Engel, eds., *Rethinking Leadership and "Whole of Government" National Security Reform: Problems, Progress, and Prospects*, Carlisle, PA, Strategic Studies Institute, 2010, pp. 49-71, p. 56.

16. Todd L. Pittinsky, Chapter 8, "Winning Hearts and Minds: From Slogan to Leadership Strategy," in Joseph R. Cerami and Jeffrey A. Engel, eds., *Rethinking Leadership and "Whole of Government" National Security Reform: Problems, Progress, and Prospects,* Carlisle, PA, Strategic Studies Institute, 2010, pp. 165-185, p. 166.

17. Andrew Preston, Chapter 6, "A Fine Balance: The Evolution of the National Security Adviser," in Joseph R. Cerami and Jeffrey A. Engel, eds., *Rethinking Leadership and "Whole of Government" National Security Reform: Problems, Progress, and Prospects,* Carlisle, PA, Strategic Studies Institute, 2010, pp. 127-147, p. 127.

18. *Ibid.,* p. 141.

19. *Ibid.,* p. 127.

20. *Ibid.,* p. 131.

21. Dean Acheson, *Present at the Creation: My Years in the State Department,* New York: W. W. Norton, 1969, epigraph and p. xviii.

ABOUT THE CONTRIBUTORS

JOSEPH R. CERAMI is a Senior Lecturer in National Security Policy and Director of the Public Service Leadership Program for the Bush School of Government and Public Service, Texas A&M University. His last U.S. Army assignment was as the Chairman of the Department of National Security and Strategy at the U.S. Army War College, Carlisle, Pennsylvania, from 1998 to 2001. From 1993 to 1998, he served on the faculty there as Director of International Security Studies. He was Assistant Professor of Political Science at the U.S. Military Academy, West Point, New York, where he taught International Relations, and Politics and Government. Along with Colonel (Ret.) James F. Holcomb, Jr., Dr. Cerami is coeditor of the *U. S.Army War College Guide to Strategy*. He is also the co-editor of *The Interagency and Counterinsurgency Warfare* (2007) and *Leadership and National Security Reform: The Next President's Agenda* (2008), both published by the Strategic Studies Institute. Dr. Cerami holds a B.S. in engineering from the U.S. Military Academy at West Point, an M.A. in government from the University of Texas at Austin, an MMAS in theater operations from the School of Advanced Military Studies at Fort Leavenworth, Kansas, and a Ph.D. in public administration from the Penn State School of Public Affairs. He is a graduate of the Army War College. In 1995 he was awarded a certificate from the John F. Kennedy School of Government, Harvard University, Program for Senior Officials in National Security.

JEFFREY A. ENGEL is an Associate Professor and Verlin and Howard Kruse '52 Founders Professor and the Director of Programming, Scowcroft Institute of

International Affairs at the Bush School of Texas A&M University. Before coming to the Bush School, he was an Olin Postdoctoral Fellow at Yale University, and a lecturer in history and international relations at the University of Pennsylvania. Dr. Engel is the author of *Cold War at 30,000 Feet: The Anglo-American Fight for Aviation Supremacy* (Harvard University Press, 2007, awarded the 2008 Paul Birdsall Prize by the American Historical Association), and edited *Local Consequences of the Global Cold War* (Stanford University Press, 2008); *The China Diary of George H. W. Bush: The Making of a Global President* (Princeton University Press, 2008); and *The Fall of the Berlin Wall: The Revolutionary Legacy of 1989* (Oxford University Press, 2009). A member of the editorial board of *Diplomatic History* and of the Executive Council of the Transatlantic Studies Association, he is currently writing *Seeking Monsters to Destroy: Language and War from Thomas Jefferson to George W. Bush* (Oxford University Press, forthcoming). Dr. Engel is a graduate of Cornell University, studied at St. Catherine's College, Oxford University, and holds a Ph.D. in American history from the University of Wisconsin-Madison.

JAMES R. LOCHER III, has worked in the White House, Pentagon, and Senate. He served as the senior staff member on the Senate Armed Services Committee for the Goldwater-Nichols Defense Reorganization Act and later for the Cohen-Nunn Amendment that created the U.S. Special Operations Command. In the first Bush and early Clinton administrations, Mr. Locher served as the assistant secretary of defense for special operations and low-intensity conflict. In 2003-04, he chaired the Defense Reform Commission in Bosnia and Herzegovina that successfully merged the three warring factions into a single military establishment and began the move toward a single army. Currently, he is the executive director of the nonpartisan Project on National Security Reform, which was established to assist the nation in reforming its national security system to meet the challenges of the 21st century. Mr. Locher is a graduate of West Point (Class of 1968) and Harvard Business School.

GEOFFREY S. FRENCH is the Analytic Director for Security Risk at CENTRA Technology, Inc., and currently supports a number of programs for the U.S. Department of Homeland Security (DHS). Mr. French has worked in counterintelligence and in the critical infrastructure protection community since the 1990s, supporting government agencies such as the Federal Bureau of Investigation and the U.S. Department of Defense. Mr. French has designed a number of risk methodologies for DHS, including tools for assessing the terrorism risk to infrastructure, the security risk to special events, and all-hazards risk to a region. In addition to overseeing risk methodological development, he provides subject matter expertise in cyber counterintelligence, especially in policy and guidance. He is a founding member of the Security Analysis and Risk Management Association. Mr. French has written a number of papers on threat and risk assessment and spoken at numerous conferences and academic settings. Some recent examples include: "Threat-Based Approach to Risk," presented to the Naval Postgraduate School Center for Homeland Defense and Security, June 2008; "Intelligence Analysis for Strategic Risk Assessments," in the December 2007 George Mason School of Law monograph *Elements of Risk*; "The Coming Counterrevolution in Military Affairs," presented to the International Security Studies

Program, Yale University, March 2003; and "The Terrorist Threat to the Information Infrastructure," Presentation to the National Academy of Sciences' Committee on the Internet Under Crisis Conditions, 2002. Mr. French holds a B.A. in history from Wichita State University and an M.A. in national security studies from Georgetown University.

JAMES GOLDGEIER is a senior fellow at the Council on Foreign Relations and a professor of political science and international affairs at George Washington University, where he has taught since 1994. Additionally, he served as a visiting fellow at Stanford University's Center for International Security and Cooperation and an assistant professor of government at Cornell University. In 1995-96, he was a Council on Foreign Relations International Affairs Fellow serving at the State Department and on the National Security Council staff. He has held appointments as a visiting fellow at the Brookings Institution, Whitney H. Shepardson Fellow at the Council on Foreign Relations, the Henry A. Kissinger scholar in foreign policy and international relations at the Library of Congress, a public policy scholar at the Woodrow Wilson International Center for Scholars, and a W. Glenn Campbell and Rita Ricardo-Campbell National Fellow and the Edward Teller National Fellow at the Hoover Institution. Dr. Goldgeier is the author of *Leadership Style and Soviet Foreign Policy* (Johns Hopkins, 1994, which received the Edgar Furniss book award in national and international security); and *Not Whether But When: The U.S. Decision to Enlarge NATO* (Brookings, 1999). He coauthored (with Michael McFaul) *Power and Purpose: U.S. Policy toward Russia after the Cold War* (Brookings, 2003, which received the 2004 Lepgold Prize for the best book on international relations). His most recent book (co-authored with Derek Chollet) is *America Between the Wars: From 11/9 to 9/11* (PublicAffairs 2008, named "a best book of 2008" by *Slate* and "a favorite book of 2008" by *The Daily Beast*). Dr. Goldgeier holds a Ph.D. from the University of California-Berkeley.

RICHARD H. IMMERMAN is Professor of History at Temple University and Director of its Center for the Study of Force and Diplomacy. The recipient of the Society for Historians of American Foreign Relations' Bernath Book Prize in 1983 and its Bernath Lecture Prize in 1990, he served as SHAFR's president in 2007. He received the Board of Regents Excellence in Research Award from the University of Hawaii and the Paul W. Eberman Faculty Research Award from Temple University. In 2004, he was named Temple's Edward J. Buthusiem Family Distinguished Faculty Fellow in History. Professor Immerman has published *The CIA in Guatemala: The Foreign Policy of Intervention*; *Waging Peace: How Eisenhower Shaped an Enduring Cold War Strategy* (with Robert R. Bowie); and *John Foster Dulles: Piety, Pragmatism, and Power in U.S. Foreign Policy*. His *American Empire for Liberty?* is currently in press. From September 2007 to December 2008, Professor Immerman served as Assistant Deputy Director of National Intelligence for Analytic Integrity and Standards and Analytic Ombudsman for the Office of the Director of National Intelligence.

TODD L. PITTINSKY is an Associate Professor of Public Policy at the Harvard Kennedy School, and serves as Research Director of Harvard's Center for Public Leadership. His recent research includes the edited volume *Crossing the Divide: Intergroup Leader-*

ship in a World of Difference (Harvard Business School Press, 2009). Through the Allophilia Project, he investigates positive intergroup attitudes, the conditions under which they develop, and how they shape the ways we think, feel, and behave. Dr. Pittinsky's current research focuses on intergroup leadership. Dr. Pittinsky holds an A.B. in psychology from Yale, an M.A. in psychology, and a Ph.D. in organizational behavior from Harvard.

ANDREW PRESTON is a Senior Lecturer in History and Fellow of Clare College at Cambridge University. He is also a Fellow at the Cold War Studies Centre at the London School of Economics, and has previously held professorships in history and international studies at Yale University; the University of Victoria, Canada; and The Graduate Institute of International and Development Studies, Geneva. In addition to several journal articles and book chapters, Mr. Preston is the author of *The War Council: McGeorge Bundy, the NSC, and Vietnam* (Harvard University Press, 2006) and co-editor, with Fredrik Logevall, of *Nixon in the World: American Foreign Relations, 1969-1977* (Oxford University Press, 2008). He is currently writing a book on the religious influence on American war and diplomacy from the colonial era to the present, to be published by Knopf.

JOEL H. ROSENTHAL is President of the Carnegie Council for Ethics in International Affairs. The Council is one of Andrew Carnegie's original peace endowments. It was founded in 1914 to promote the principles of pluralism and peace. Under Dr. Rosenthal's direction, the Council sponsors educational programs for worldwide audiences. The Council's lectures, publications, and educational programs focus on issues relating to ethics and war, the global economy, and cultural difference. He also serves as Senior Fellow, Stockdale Center, U.S. Naval Academy; Adjunct Professor, New York University; and Chairman of the Bard College Globalization and International Affairs Program in New York City. Dr. Rosenthal is editor-in-chief of the journal *Ethics & International Affairs* and the author of *Righteous Realists.* He has coedited several collections of articles and written numerous articles of his own including "Ethics" in Bruce W. Jentleson *et al., Encyclopedia of US Foreign Relations.* His work in progress includes *How Moral Can We Get? Essays on the Moral Nation.* Dr. Rosenthal holds a B.A. from Harvard University and a Ph.D. from Yale University.

J. ETHAN BENNETT is a current student at the Bush School of Government and Public Service at Texas A&M University. Mr. Bennett's focus on Latin America brought him to South America, where he twice served as an English teacher to Chilean high school students in Valparaíso and Quilpué, Chile. He is currently pursuing a master's degree in international affairs, and has concentrations in national Security studies and international economics. Mr. Bennett has a triple major in Spanish, Latin American studies, and international economics from the University of Kentucky.

THE GEORGE BUSH SCHOOL OF GOVERNMENT AND PUBLIC SERVICE, TEXAS A&M UNIVERSITY

The George Bush School of Government and Public Service, Texas A&M University, educates principled leaders in public and international affairs, conducts research, and performs service. Both the Master of Public Service and Administration (MPSA) and Master's Program in International Affairs (MPIA) are full-time graduate degree programs that provide a professional education for individuals seeking careers in the public or nonprofit sectors, or for activities in the private sector that have a governmental focus.

The MPSA, a 21-month, 48-credit-hour program, combines 11 courses in public management, policy analysis, economics, and research methods with five electives. Students select an elective concentration in one of the following areas: nonprofit organizations; state and local policy and management; natural resources, environment, and technology policy and administration; security, energy, and technology policy; and health policy and management. A professional internship is completed in the first summer session.

The MPIA, a 21-month, 48-credit-hour program, offers tracks in National Security Affairs and International Economics and Development. Students construct a program of study based on two or more concentrations or clusters of related courses such as economic development, diplomacy in world affairs, intelligence in statecraft, national security, or regional studies. Satisfactory completion of a foreign language exam is required to graduate. At the end of their first year of study, students will participate in either an internationally oriented internship or a foreign language immersion course.

The Certificate in Advanced International Affairs (CAIA) program is a focused curriculum offered via distance education or through in-residence study. The program consists of 12-15 credit hours of graduate courses designed for those with limited time but a strong desire to upgrade specific dimensions of their international relations background. In addition, the School offers certificate programs in Homeland Security (online), China Studies (in-residence), Nonprofit Management (online or in-residence), and National Security (executive education).

More information on the Bush School is available from *bush.tamu.edu/*.

THE SCOWCROFT INSTITUTE OF INTERNATIONAL AFFAIRS

The Scowcroft Institute of International Affairs (SIIA) is a research institute housed in the Bush School of Government and Public Service, Texas A&M University. The Institute is named in honor of Lieutenant General Brent Scowcroft, USAF (Ret.), whose long and distinguished career in public service included serving as National Security Advisor for Presidents Gerald Ford and George H. W. Bush. The Institute's core mission is to foster and disseminate policy-oriented research on international affairs by supporting faculty and student research, hosting international speakers and major scholarly conferences, and providing grants to outside researchers to use the holdings of the Bush Library.

THE STRATEGIC STUDIES INSTITUTE

The Strategic Studies Institute (SSI) is the U.S. Army's center for geostrategic and national security research and analysis. SSI conducts strategic research and analysis to support the U.S. Army War College curriculum, provides direct analysis for Army and Department of Defense (DoD) leadership, and serves as a bridge to the wider strategic community.

SSI is composed of civilian research professors, uniformed military officers, and a professional support staff. All have extensive credentials and experience. SSI is divided into three components: the Strategic Research and Analysis Department focuses on global, trans-regional, and functional issues, particularly those dealing with Army transformation; the Regional Strategy Department focuses on regional strategic issues; and the Academic Engagement Program creates and sustains partnerships with the global strategic community. In addition to its organic resources, SSI has a web of partnerships with strategic analysts around the world, including the foremost thinkers in the field of security and military strategy. In most years, about half of SSI's publications are written by these external partners.

SSI documents are published by the Institute and distributed to key strategic leaders in the Army and the DoD, the military educational system, Congress, the news media, other think tanks and defense institutes, and major colleges and universities. SSI publications use history and current political, economic, and military factors to develop strategic recommendations.

- Books - SSI publishes about 3-5 books per year consisting of authored works or edited compilations.
- Monographs – Policy-oriented reports provide recommendations. They are usually 25-90 pages in length.
- Carlisle Papers - The best of the student papers submitted in compliance with requirements for graduation from the U.S. Army War College are highlighted.
- LeTort Papers - Essays, retrospectives, or speeches of interest to the defense academic community comprise this category.
- Colloquium Reports - For larger conferences, SSI may produce a report on the proceedings.
- Colloquium Briefs - These 2 to 4-page briefs are produced after the colloquia with which SSI has co-sponsored or helped to fund.

At the request of the Army leadership, SSI sometimes provides shorter analytical reports on pressing strategic issues. The distribution of these is usually limited.

Additionally, every year SSI compiles a Key Strategic Issues List (KSIL) based on input from the U.S. Army War College faculty, the Army Staff, the Joint Staff, the unified and specified commands, and other Army organizations. This is designed to guide the research of SSI, the U.S. Army War College, and other Army-related strategic analysts.

SSI analysts publish widely outside of the Institute's own products. They have written books for Cambridge University Press, Princeton University Press, University Press of Kansas, Duke University Press, Praeger, Frank Cass, Rowman and Littlefield, and Brassey's. They have contributed chapters to many other books including publications from the Brookings Institution, Jane's Defence Group, and the Center for Strategic and International Studies. SSI analysts have written articles for such journals as *Foreign Affairs, International Security, Survival, Washington Quarterly, Orbis, The National Interest, Current History, Political Science Quarterly, Joint Force Quarterly, Parameters, The Journal of Politics, Security Studies, Journal of Strategic Studies, Jane's Intelligence Review, Occasional Papers of the Woodrow Wilson Center, Contemporary Security Policy, Defense Analysis, Military Operations Research, Strategic Review, Military Review, National Security Studies Quarterly, Journal of Military History, War in History, War & Society, The Historian, Infantry Magazine, The World and I, Aerospace Historian, Central Asian Security, Asian Survey, SAIS Review, China Quarterly, Comparative Politics, Journal of Political and Military Sociology, Small Wars and Insurgencies, Georgetown Journal of International Affairs, Special Warfare, Comparative Strategy, Korean Journal of Defense Analysis, Journal of East Asian Studies, World Affairs, Problems of Post-Communism, Conflict, Diplomatic History, Airpower Journal, Low Intensity Conflict and Law Enforcement, Politique Étranger, Allgemeine Schweizerische Militärzeitschrift,* and *African Security Review.*

SSI also co-sponsors academic conferences to examine issues of importance to the Army, collaborating with some of the leading universities in the country. Recent partners include Georgetown, Princeton, Harvard, MIT, Columbia, University of Chicago, University of Miami, Stanford, Georgia Tech, Johns Hopkins, and the Bush School of Government and Public Service at Texas A&M University.

U.S. ARMY WAR COLLEGE

Major General Robert M. Williams
Commandant

*****

STRATEGIC STUDIES INSTITUTE

Director
Professor Douglas C. Lovelace, Jr.

Director of Research
Dr. Antulio J. Echevarria II

Editors
Dr. Joseph R. Cerami
Dr. Jeffrey A. Engel

Director of Publications
Dr. James G. Pierce

Publications Assistant
Ms. Rita A. Rummel

*****

Composition
Helen Musser

www.ingramcontent.com/pod-product-compliance
Lightning Source LLC
Chambersburg PA
CBHW081358270326
41930CB00015B/3345